# Math Contests—Grades 4, 5, and 6
## Volume 2

School Years: 1986-87 through 1990-91

Steven R. Conrad ● Daniel Flegler

Published by MATH LEAGUE PRESS
Printed in the United States of America

# And the winning number...

Cover art by Bob DeRosa

Second Printing (revised), 1994

Math League Press
P.O. Box 720
Tenafly, NJ 07670

ISBN 0-940805-03-0

# Preface

*The 2nd Math Contest Book for Grades 4, 5, and 6* is the second volume in our series of problem books for students in these grades. The first volume contained the contests that were given from the 1979-80 school year through the 1985-86 school year. (A form you may use to order any of our books appears on page 102.) This volume contains the contests that were given from 1986-87 through 1990-91.

This book is divided into three sections for ease of use by both students and teachers. The first section of the book contains the contests. Each contest is a 30- or 40-question multiple-choice contest that can be worked in a 30-minute period. Each of the 3-page contests is designed so that questions on the 1st page are generally straightforward, those on the 2nd page are moderate in difficulty, and those on the 3rd page are more difficult. The second section of the book consists of detailed solutions to all the contest questions. The third and final section of the book consists of the letter answers to each contest and rating scales to evaluate individual performance.

Many people may prefer to consult the answer section rather than the solution section when first reviewing a contest. It is the experience of the authors that reworking a problem when the answer (but *not* the solution) is known frequently leads to increased understanding of problem-solving techniques.

Until the 1988-89 school year, we offered a single contest known as the Annual Elementary Grades Mathematics Contest. Prior to that time, any student in grade 6 or below was eligible to participate in this contest. Since the 1988-89 school year, we have sponsored three annual contests: The Annual 4th Grade Mathematics Contest, the Annual 5th Grade Mathematics Contest, and the Annual 6th Grade Mathematics Contest. A student may participate in the contest designed for his/her current grade level or for any higher grade level. For example, students in grades 4 and 5 (or below) are eligible to participate in the 6th Grade Contest.

Steven R. Conrad & Daniel Flegler, contest authors

i

# Acknowledgments

For her continued patience and understanding, special thanks to Marina Conrad, whose only mathematical skill, an important one, is the ability to count the ways.

For her lifetime support and encouragement, special thanks to Mildred Flegler.

To Alan Feldman, who suggested several stylistic changes from the first volume to this one, we offer our thanks.

To Paul Ericksen and Mark Motyka, we offer our gratitude for their assistance over the years.

To Brian and Keith Conrad, who did an awesome proofreading job, thanks!

# Table Of Contents

# 1988-89 Annual 4th Grade Contest

*Spring, 1989*

**4**

## Instructions

- **Time** You will have only *30 minutes* working time for this contest. You might be *unable* to finish all 30 questions in the time allowed.

- **Scores** Remember *this is a contest, not a test.* There is no "passing" or "failing" score. Few students score as high as 24 points (80% correct); students with even half that, 12 points, *deserve commendation!*

- **Format and Point Value** This is a multiple-choice contest. For each question, write the *capital letter* that is *in front of* the answer you choose. For each question, your answer will be one of the *capital letters* A, B, C, or D. Each question you answer correctly is worth 1 point. Unanswered questions receive no credit.

| | | Answer Column |
|---|---|---|
| 1. | $19 + 89 =$ <br> A) 1989    B) 918    C) 108    D) 98 | 1. |
| 2. | The 24th letter of our alphabet is <br> A) *w*    B) *x*    C) *y*    D) *z* | 2. |
| 3. | $(1 + 2 + 3 + 4 + 5) - (5 + 4 + 3 + 2 + 1) =$ <br> A) 0    B) 2    C) 15    D) 30 | 3. |
| 4. | Which of the following is *not* a whole number? <br> A) 6 + 5    B) 6–5    C) 6 × 5    D) 6 ÷ 5 | 4. |
| 5. | The product of 9 and 221 is    就是 9 × 221 <br> A) 230    B) 1899    C) 1989    D) 1999 | 5. |
| 6. | $(99 \times 10) + (99 \times 1) =$ <br> A) 209    B) 999    C) 1089    D) 1099 | 6. |
| 7. | What number is 2 less than the number which is 3 more than 99? <br> A) 94    B) 98    C) 100    D) 104 | 7. |
| 8. | $100 \times 10 \times 1 \times 0 =$ <br> A) 1110    B) 1000    C) 111    D) 0 | 8. |
| 9. | If a math teacher divides 1234 by 56, what would be the *sum* of the quotient and the remainder that the teacher should get? <br> A) 2    B) 20    C) 22    D) 24 | 9. |
| 10. | If Lee multiplied 121 by itself, the result would be <br> A) 14641    B) 484    C) 242    D) 121 | 10. |
| 11. | Pat's teacher is 26 years older than Pat. Pat is 9. How old is Pat's teacher? <br> A) 34    B) 35    C) 36    D) 37 | 11. |

*Go on to the next page* ▐▐▶ **4**

12. $9 + 80 + 700 + 6000 =$

    A) 6789     B) 6798     C) 9876     D) 30000

12.

13. 1 hundred + 11 tens + 111 ones =

    A) 123     B) 222     C) 321     D) 1221

13.

14. By what number must you multiply 30 to get the product 3000?

    A) 10     B) 100     C) 300     D) 1000

14.

15. A whole number is multiplied by 16. The product could *never* be

    A) 0     B) 48     C) 72     D) 80

15.

16. $(50 \times 30) + (50 \times 9) + (1 \times 30) + (1 \times 9) =$

    A) $51 \times 39$     B) $50 \times 39$     C) $51 \times 30$     D) $51 \times 30 \times 9$

16.

17. A rectangle has 1 more side than a

    A) pentagon    B) circle     C) square     D) triangle

17.

18. Every one of the following is a factor of 1989 *except*

    A) 3     B) 9     C) 11     D) 221

18.

19. $5 + 10 + 15 + 20 + 25 = \underline{\ ?\ } \times (1 + 2 + 3 + 4 + 5)$

    A) 5     B) 10     C) 15     D) 25

19.

20. A subscription to a certain comic costs $7.60 for 8 issues. If single copies cost 95¢, how much do you save by subscribing?

    A) $0.00     B) 95¢     C) $1.90     D) $3.80

20.

21. How many even whole numbers are prime numbers?

    A) 0     B) 1     C) 2     D) 3

21.

22. If the correct time now is 1:15 P.M., and if my clock stopped running three and one-half hours ago, when did it stop running?

    A) 8:45 A.M.    B) 9:45 A.M.    C) 10:45 A.M.    D) 4:45 P.M.

22.

*Go on to the next page* ▐▐▶    **4**

23. In the land of Seuss, a plate of green eggs costs twice as much as a plate of ham. If a plate of ham costs 5¢, how much would I pay for 2 plates of green eggs and 3 plates of ham?

A) 40¢          B) 35¢          C) 30¢          D) 25¢

23.

24. I can mail up to 3 school yearbooks in 1 Special Shipping Box. If I want to mail 22 school yearbooks in these Special Boxes, at least how many of these Special Shipping Boxes will I need?

A) 6          B) 7          C) 8          D) 11

24.

25. I'm thinking of two whole numbers. One of the numbers has 3 digits and the other has 2 digits. The difference between the two numbers is 1. What is the sum of these two whole numbers?

A) 100          B) 101          C) 199          D) 201

25.

26. The sum $11 + 12 + 13 + 14 + 15 + 16 + 17$ is divisible by

A) 11          B) 12          C) 13          D) 14

26.

27. Sidney the Seahorse wants to power his house with electric eels. Sidney needs 117 watts of electricity. Each eel produces 3 watts of electricity. How many eels does Sidney need?

A) 39          B) 117          C) 120          D) 351

27.

28. A certain tree trunk splits into 3 large branches. Each large branch splits into 4 small branches. Each small branch splits into 5 twigs. What is the total number of twigs on this tree?

A) 5          B) 12          C) 20          D) 60

28.

29. January 1, 1989 was a Sunday. January 1, 1990 will fall on a

A) Saturday     B) Sunday     C) Monday     D) Tuesday

29.

30. $(101 + 100 + \ldots + 3 + 2) - (100 + 99 + \ldots + 2 + 1) =$

A) 99          B) 100          C) 101          D) 102

30.

*The end of the contest* ✍

**4**

Solutions on Page 45 • Answers on Page 90

# 1989-90 Annual 4th Grade Contest

*Spring, 1990*

**4**

## Instructions

- **Time** You will have only *30 minutes* working time for this contest. You might be *unable* to finish all 30 questions in the time allowed.

- **Scores** Remember *this is a contest, not a test.* There is no "passing" or "failing" score. Few students score as high as 24 points (80% correct); students with even half that, 12 points, *deserve commendation!*

- **Format and Point Value** This is a multiple-choice contest. For each question, write the *capital letter* that is *in front of* the answer you choose. For each question, your answer will be one of the *capital letters* A, B, C, or D. Each question you answer correctly is worth 1 point. Unanswered questions receive no credit.

Copyright © 1990 by Mathematics Leagues Inc.

1.  $1 + 9 + 9 + 0 =$

    A) 10      B) 19      C) 109      D) 1990

    1.

2.  Add the number of vowels in our alphabet to the number of consonants in our alphabet. What is the sum?

    A) 26      B) 30      C) 31      D) 32

    2.

3.  $(19 \times 100) + (9 \times 10) =$

    A) 280      B) 1909      C) 1990      D) 2880

    3.

4.  Which number is twenty-three more than forty-nine?

    A) 72      B) 62      C) 26      D) 16

    4.

5.  $10 + 11 + 12 + 13 + 14 = 11 + 12 + 13 + 14 + \underline{\ ?\ }$

    A) 15      B) 14      C) 12      D) 10

    5.

6.  If Ronnie has 12 *pairs* of shoes, how many shoes does Ronnie have?

    A) 6      B) 12      C) 14      D) 24

    6.

7.  $1 + 11 + 111 + 1111 =$

    A) 11111      B) 1111      C) 4321      D) 1234

    7.

8.  When twice 24 is divided by half of 8, what is the result?

    A) 3      B) 6      C) 12      D) 18

    8.

9.  $777 + 888 + 999 =$

    A) 2664      B) 2554      C) 2464      D) 2444

    9.

10. The Smith family went out for dinner. Each of the two parents' meals cost $10. Each of the three children ordered the $3 special children's meal. How much did these meals cost (not including tax and tip)?

    A) $13      B) $23      C) $29      D) $36

    10.

11. Which of the following is equal to 0?

    A) $5 + 5$      B) $5 - 5$      C) $5 \times 5$      D) $5 \div 5$

    11.

*Go on to the next page* ⟶ **4**

| | |
|---|---|
| 12. $(1 \div 1) \times (2 \div 2) \times (3 \div 3) \times (4 \div 4) =$ <br><br> A) 1      B) 4      C) 10      D) 24 | 12. |
| 13. Each time Joel's phone rings, it rings for 3 seconds, then it's silent for 2 seconds. If Joel's phone rings 5 times, how much time does it take from the beginning of the first ring until the end of the final ring? <br><br> A) 15 seconds   B) 17 seconds   C) 23 seconds   D) 25 seconds | 13. |
| 14. $(2 + 4 + 6 + 8) \div (1 + 2 + 3 + 4) =$ <br><br> A) 20      B) 10      C) 4      D) 2 | 14. |
| 15. Multiply the number of sides of a triangle by the number of sides of a square. What is the product? <br><br> A) 7      B) 8      C) 12      D) 16 | 15. |
| 16. What is the average of 24, 48, and 96? <br><br> A) 48      B) 52      C) 55      D) 56 | 16. |
| 17. The first odd whole number is 1, the second is 3, and so on. What is the tenth odd whole number? <br><br> A) 21      B) 19      C) 17      D) 11 | 17. |
| 18. If Lee has 1 quarter, 2 dimes, and 1 penny, how much money does Lee have? <br><br> A) 36¢      B) 37¢      C) 46¢      D) 61¢ | 18. |
| 19. A piece of string is 3 m long. It is cut into pieces that are each 30 cm long. Into how many pieces is it cut? <br><br> A) 3      B) 10      C) 90      D) 100 | 19. |
| 20. What is the greatest common factor of 36 and 90? <br><br> A) 3      B) 9      C) 18      D) 90 | 20. |
| 21. A line and a circle are drawn on a piece of paper so that the line passes through the center of the circle. How many times does the line cross the circle? <br><br> A) 0      B) 1      C) 2      D) 3 | 21. |

*Go on to the next page* ▐▌▐▌➡ **4**

| | | |
|---|---|---|
| 22. | Dale read all the pages in a chapter of a book, starting with page 20 and finishing with page 40. How many pages did Dale read?<br><br>A) 40      B) 21      C) 20      D) 19 | 22. |
| 23. | What time will it be 53 minutes past 11:15 A.M.?<br><br>A) 12:08 P.M.   B) 12:13 P.M.   C) 1:03 P.M.   D) 12:08 A.M. | 23. |
| 24. | Which of these products has the smallest one's digit?<br><br>A) 3×6×7×8×9×11      B) 11×21×31×41×51<br>C) 15×25×35×45      D) 11×22×33×44×55 | 24. |
| 25. | Gerry has five coins. Only one of these coins is a penny. What is the least amount of money Gerry can have?<br><br>A) 5¢      B) 16¢      C) 21¢      D) 42¢ | 25. |
| 26. | Mary is 2 years younger than John. In 3 years, John will be 10 years old. How old is Mary now?<br><br>A) 8      B) 7      C) 6      D) 5 | 26. |
| 27. | If apples are only sold in packages of 4, what is the least number of packages I must buy to get 26 apples?<br><br>A) 6      B) 7      C) 8      D) 12 | 27. |
| 28. | If today were Monday, the day after tomorrow would be<br><br>A) Wednesday   B) Thursday    C) Friday     D) Saturday | 28. |
| 29. | Pat paints twice as fast as Lee. If it took Lee 6 hours to paint a room, how long would it have taken if both had painted the room together?<br><br>A) 2 hours    B) 3 hours    C) 9 hours    D) 18 hours | 29. |
| 30. | How many different 3-digit whole numbers have all of the numbers 1, 2, and 3 as their digits?<br><br>A) 3      B) 6      C) 123      D) 300 | 30. |

*The end of the contest* ✍🏻    **4**

Solutions on Page 49 • Answers on Page 91

# 1990-91 Annual 4th Grade Contest

*Spring, 1991*

**4**

## Instructions

- **Time** You will have only *30 minutes* working time for this contest. You might be *unable* to finish all 30 questions in the time allowed.

- **Scores** Remember *this is a contest, not a test*. There is no "passing" or "failing" score. Few students score as high as 24 points (80% correct); students with even half that, 12 points, *deserve commendation!*

- **Format and Point Value** This is a multiple-choice contest. For each question, write the *capital letter* that is *in front of* the answer you choose. For each question, your answer will be one of the *capital letters* A, B, C, or D. Each question you answer correctly is worth 1 point. Unanswered questions receive no credit.

1. $19 + 91 =$

   A) 100          B) 101          C) 110          D) 1991

2. How many 3¢ stamps can you buy with 21¢?

   A) 7            B) 18           C) 24           D) 63

3. $1 \times (1 + 1) \times (1 + 1 + 1) =$

   A) 1            B) 3            C) 5            D) 6

4. What is the value of 9898 rounded to the nearest ten?

   A) 9800         B) 9890         C) 9900         D) 9990

5. $1234 + 4321 =$

   A) 4444         B) 4567         C) 4765         D) 5555

6. Find the missing number: $8 \times 8 = 64 \times \underline{?}$

   A) 1            B) 2            C) 4            D) 64

7. In square ABCD shown at the right, $AB = 3$. What is the perimeter of this square?

   A) 3            B) 6            C) 9            D) 12

8. 25 nickels $= \underline{?}$ quarters

   A) 1            B) 5            C) 25           D) 125

9. $12 \div (5 - 2) =$

   A) 1            B) 3            C) 4            D) 9

10. Which of the following is an even number?

    A) 1234        B) 4321         C) 2413         D) 4231

11. $(1 \times 100) + (10 \times 10) + (100 \times 1) =$

    A) 100         B) 111          C) 220          D) 300

12. Of the following, which has *exactly* 3 positive factors?

    A) 1           B) 3            C) 4            D) 6

*Go on to the next page* ▥➡ **4**

Answer Column

| | | |
|---|---|---|
| 13. $25 + 25 + 25 + 25 + 25 =$ <br> A) $25 \times 25$   B) $25 + 5$   C) $25 \div 5$   D) $25 \times 5$ | 13. |
| 14. In New York, if I travel 1 km north, then 1 km east, then 1 km south, how far am I from where I started? <br> A) 0 km   B) 1 km   C) 2 km   D) 3 km | 14. |
| 15. $(3 + 3) \times (3 - 3) \times (3 \div 3) =$ <br> A) 0   B) 3   C) 6   D) 9 | 15. |
| 16. If four times a number is 20, what is two times that same number? <br> A) 5   B) 10   C) 20   D) 40 | 16. |
| 17. $2 \times 2 \times 2 \times 5 \times 5 \times 5 =$ <br> A) 100   B) 200   C) 500   D) 1000 | 17. |
| 18. Find the ones' digit in the following sum: $999 + 999 + 999$. <br> A) 2   B) 7   C) 8   D) 9 | 18. |
| 19. $123 + 231 + 312 =$ <br> A) 456   B) 555   C) 567   D) 666 | 19. |
| 20. The product of two whole numbers is 5. What is the sum of these two numbers? <br> A) 10   B) 6   C) 5   D) 4 | 20. |
| 21. A newspaper store is open from 7 A.M. until 8 P.M. every day. For how many hours is this store open each day? <br> A) 8   B) 12   C) 13   D) 15 | 21. |
| 22. $111 \times 111 =$ <br> A) 11111   B) 12321   C) 12345   D) 14641 | 22. |
| 23. The sum of the ages of Tom, Dick, and Harry is 26. If Tom is 9 and Dick is 10, how old is Harry? <br> A) 7   B) 11   C) 16   D) 17 | 23. |

*Go on to the next page* ⫸  **4**

11

24. What is the largest whole number which, when multiplied by 3, is less than 25?

   A) 7          B) 8          C) 9          D) 24

   24.

25. There are two whole numbers each less than 100 whose sum is 197. What is the difference between these two numbers?

   A) 0          B) 1          C) 2          D) 3

   25.

26. The running time of the film *The Jungle Book* is 1 hour and 18 minutes. If the film begins at 1:45 P.M. and is shown without any interruptions, at what time will *The Jungle Book* end?

   A) 2:03 P.M.    B) 2:18 P.M.    C) 3:03 P.M.    D) 3:18 P.M.

   26.

27. 98 + 99 + 100 + 101 + 102 =

   A) 497         B) 498         C) 499         D) 500

   27.

28. I have 17¢. If I double the number of pennies I have, I would then have 29¢. How many pennies do I have?

   A) 12          B) 7          C) 5          D) 2

   28.

29. When the hour hand of a circular clock goes around once, the minute hand goes around

   A) 12 times    B) 24 times    C) 60 times    D) 720 times

   29.

30. How many different triangles are there altogether in the diagram at the right? (Two triangles are different if *at least* one vertex is different.)

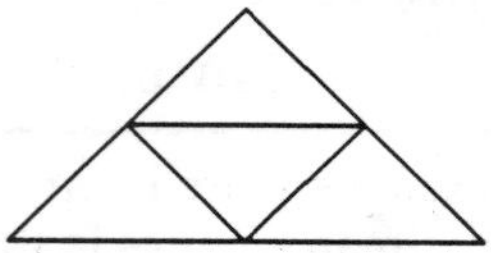

   A) 1          B) 4          C) 5          D) 6

   30.

*The end of the contest* ✍️    **4**

Solutions on Page 53 • Answers on Page 92

# 1988-89 Annual 5th Grade Contest

*Spring, 1989*

**5**

## Instructions

- **Time**  You will have only *30 minutes* working time for this contest. You might be *unable* to finish all 30 questions in the time allowed.

- **Scores**  Remember *this is a contest, not a test.* There is no "passing" or "failing" score. Few students score as high as 24 points (80% correct); students with even half that, 12 points, *deserve commendation!*

- **Format and Point Value**  This is a multiple-choice contest. For each question, write the *capital letter* that is *in front of* the answer you choose. For each question, your answer will be one of the *capital letters* A, B, C, or D. Each question you answer correctly is worth 1 point. Unanswered questions receive no credit.

1. $1989 = 9 \times \underline{\ ?\ }$

   A) 111      B) 121      C) 211      D) 221

   1.

2. Each of the following has the value 0 *except*

   A) $0 + 100$    B) $0 \times 100$    C) $0 \div 100$    D) $100 - 100$

   2.

3. $1 \times 1 \times 1 \times 1 \times 9 \times 1 \times 1 \times 1 \times 1 =$

   A) 9      B) 17      C) 72      D) 81

   3.

4. Of the following, which is closest in value to 1989?

   A) 989      B) 1889      C) 1970      D) 2000

   4.

5. $98 + 98 + 98 + 98 + 98 + 2 + 2 + 2 + 2 + 2 =$

   A) 495      B) 500      C) 505      D) 999

   5.

6. Pat has 10 pennies and 10 nickels. The value of these coins is

   A) 20¢      B) 50¢      C) 60¢      D) $1.10

   6.

7. $4321 + 5678 =$

   A) 9889      B) 9009      C) 10009      D) 9999

   7.

8. A string of length 12 is cut into 3 pieces of equal length. What is the sum of the lengths of the 3 pieces?

   A) 3      B) 4      C) 9      D) 12

   8.

9. $(2 + 3 + 4 + 5 + 6 + 7 + 8 + 9) - (8 + 7 + 6 + 5 + 4 + 3 + 2) =$

   A) 0      B) 1      C) 9      D) 79

   9.

10. How many of the whole numbers from 1 to 100 are divisible by 3?

    A) 3      B) 30      C) 33      D) 34

    10.

11. What is the square of 4?

    A) 2      B) 8      C) 16      D) 44

    11.

*Go on to the next page* ⠿➡ **5**

12. Today, the difference between my parents' ages is 10 years. Four years ago, what was the difference between their ages?

    A) 2 years     B) 6 years     C) 10 years     D) 14 years

    12.

13. $99 + 99 + 99 + 99 + 99 + 99 + 99 + 99 + 99 + 99 =$

    A) $10 \times 99$     B) $10 + 99$     C) $9 \times 99$     D) $99 \times 99$

    13.

14. The Speedo Car Co. charges $8400 for a car, but gives a $600 rebate. (A rebate is a return of money to the buyer.) What is real cost of the car, *after* the rebate but *before* taxes?

    A) $2400     B) $7800     C) $8400     D) $9000

    14.

15. $12 \times 34 + 56 \div 7 =$

    A) $464 \div 7$     B) $1080 \div 7$     C) $504$     D) $416$

    15.

16. When 1 is added to an even number, the new number must be

    A) prime          B) divisible by 3
    C) even           D) odd

    16.

17. If a phone call costs 20¢ for the first 3 minutes and 5¢ for each additional minute, what is the cost of a 10-minute call?

    A) 25¢     B) 55¢     C) 65¢     D) 95¢

    17.

18. What is the average of 1, 2, 3, 4, 5, 6, and 7?

    A) 1     B) 4     C) 7     D) 28

    18.

19. $1000 \times 100 \times 10 \times 1 \times 0.1 \times 0.01 \times 0.001 =$

    A) 0     B) 0.1     C) 1     D) 10

    19.

20. Which of the following has the same number of sides as a rectangle?

    A) a triangle     B) a rhombus     C) a circle     D) a pentagon

    20.

21. $12 : 3 = 20 : \underline{\ ?\ }$

    A) 4     B) 5     C) 6     D) 8

    21.

*Go on to the next page* ▮▮▶  **5**

| | |
|---|---|
| 22. How many positive prime numbers have a ones' digit of 5?<br><br>A) 0      B) 1      C) 5      D) 25 | 22. |
| 23. A movie projector works by showing 32 different "frames" every second. What is the number of "frames" in a one-hour movie?<br><br>A) 3600    B) 32 × 60    C) 32 × 360    D) 32 × 3600 | 23. |
| 24. Of the following, which fraction does *not* equal $\frac{2}{3}$?<br><br>A) $\frac{22}{33}$      B) $\frac{20}{30}$      C) $\frac{4}{6}$      D) $\frac{12}{13}$ | 24. |
| 25. The tens' digit of a two-digit number is 5. Round this number to the nearest hundred.<br><br>A) 0      B) 50      C) 100      D) 150 | 25. |
| 26. As shown, square *ABCD* has side-length 4, and *BEC* is an equilateral triangle. The perimeter of the shaded figure *ABECD* is<br><br>A) 16      B) 20      C) 24      D) 28 | 26. |
| 27. The *digital sum* for the year 1989 is $1 + 9 + 8 + 9$ or 27. How many years from 1990 to 2800 have a *digital sum* of 27?<br><br>A) 0      B) 1      C) 2      D) 3 | 27. |
| 28. If I start with $100, increase this by 50%, then decrease the new amount by 50%, how much money will I have?<br><br>A) $50      B) $66      C) $75      D) $100 | 28. |
| 29. What is the correct time 3600 seconds before 1:30 P.M.?<br><br>A) 12:30 P.M.   B) 2:30 P.M.   C) 7:30 P.M.   D) 1:30 A.M. | 29. |
| 30. Jamuary 1, 1989 was a Sunday. January 1, 1988 (a leap year) was<br><br>A) a Friday    B) a Saturday   C) a Sunday   D) a Monday | 30. |

*The end of the contest* ✍️ **5**

Solutions on Page 57 • Answers on Page 93

# 1989-90 Annual 5th Grade Contest

*Spring, 1990*

**5**

## Instructions

- **Time** You will have only *30 minutes* working time for this contest. You might be *unable* to finish all 30 questions in the time allowed.

- **Scores** Remember *this is a contest, not a test.* There is no "passing" or "failing" score. Few students score as high as 24 points (80% correct); students with even half that, 12 points, *deserve commendation!*

- **Format and Point Value** This is a multiple-choice contest. For each question, write the *capital letter* that is *in front of* the answer you choose. For each question, your answer will be one of the *capital letters* A, B, C, or D. Each question you answer correctly is worth 1 point. Unanswered questions receive no credit.

Answer Column

1. $1000 + 900 + 90 + 0 =$

   A) 2000      B) 1990      C) 199      D) 0

   1.

2. I have 1 penny, 5 nickels, and 10 dimes. How much money do I have?

   A) $1.25      B) $1.26      C) $1.51      D) $1.60

   2.

3. $5 + (5 \times 5) - (5 \div 5) =$

   A) 29      B) 25      C) 23      D) 9

   3.

4. The numeral 1990 has 4 digits. How many digits are there in the numeral for one million?

   A) one million  B) ten      C) seven      D) six

   4.

5. When 1992 is divided by 1990, the remainder is

   A) 1      B) 2      C) 1990      D) 1992

   5.

6. $3000 = 30 \times \underline{\ ?\ }$

   A) 10      B) 30      C) 100      D) 300

   6.

7. What is the sum of nine eights and eight nines?

   A) 72      B) 144      C) 187      D) 9889

   7.

8. $(45 + 45 + 45 + 45 + 45) + (55 + 55 + 55 + 55 + 55) =$

   A) 400      B) 450      C) 500      D) 555

   8.

9. Which of the following numbers is divisible by 3?

   A) 49      B) 50      C) 51      D) 52

   9.

10. $1919 \div 19 =$

    A) 10      B) 11      C) 100      D) 101

    10.

11. What is the product of all four digits in the year 1990?

    A) 0      B) 1      C) 19      D) 81

    11.

12. What is the sum of the first four positive *prime* numbers?

    A) 10      B) 11      C) 16      D) 17

    12.

*Go on to the next page* ➠ **5**

| | |
|---|---|
| 13. 2 + 22 + 222 + 2222 = <br><br> A) 2468     B) 4444     C) 8642     D) 8888 | 13. |
| 14. Jack was supposed to meet Jill at 2:13 P.M. If Jill arrived 20 minutes early, then Jill arrived at <br><br> A) 1:43 P.M.    B) 1:47 P.M.    C) 1:53 P.M.    D) 1:57 P.M. | 14. |
| 15. 15 + 15 + 15 + 15 + 15 = 5 × <u>?</u> <br><br> A) 75     B) 15     C) 12     D) 3 | 15. |
| 16. The product of two *consecutive* whole numbers is 56. What is the *sum* of these two consecutive numbers? <br><br> A) 7     B) 11     C) 14     D) 15 | 16. |
| 17. 2 × 3 × 4 × 5 = 3 × 4 × 5 × <u>?</u> <br><br> A) 2     B) 3     C) 4     D) 6 | 17. |
| 18. Paul started with a certain number. After doubling it, Paul got a result that was exactly equal to his original number. What was the value of Paul's original number? <br><br> A) 0     B) 1     C) 2     D) 4 | 18. |
| 19. What is the average of 6, 60, and 600? <br><br> A) 666     B) 333     C) 222     D) 111 | 19. |
| 20. When Alexandra multiplied a certain whole number by itself, the product she got was 36. What was this whole number? <br><br> A) 4     B) 6     C) 9     D) 36 | 20. |
| 21. Of the following whole numbers, which has the fewest number of factors? <br><br> A) 6     B) 8     C) 10     D) 11 | 21. |
| 22. When 1990 is rounded to the nearest hundred, the result will be <br><br> A) 1900     B) 1990     C) 1995     D) 2000 | 22. |

*Go on to the next page* ⅲ➡ **5**

23. How many 2's must be multiplied together for the product to equal 64?

    A) 5          B) 6          C) 7          D) 32

24. If *YOURS* plus *MINE* is equal to *YOURS* minus *MINE*, what does *MINE* equal?

    A) 0          B) 1          C) 2          D) 10

25. If the average of three consecutive whole numbers is 24, what is the largest of these three whole numbers?

    A) 22         B) 24         C) 25         D) 26

26. The sum of the ages of both of my parents now is 70. Six years ago, the sum of their ages was

    A) 58         B) 64         C) 70         D) 76

27. On a class test, everyone took the test and everyone got a different grade. Ali's grade was both the 10th highest grade *and* the 10th lowest grade in the class. How many students were in this class?

    A) 10         B) 19         C) 20         D) 21

28. The one's digit of the product $9 \times 9 \times 9 \times 9 \times 9 \times 9 \times 9 \times 9$ is

    A) 1          B) 2          C) 8          D) 9

29. When Joan counted backwards from 100 by 7's, she began 100, 93, 86, . . . . In this manner, Joan counted each of the following numbers *except*

    A) 65         B) 30         C) 23         D) 15

30. In how many different ways can the letters in the word *STOP* be arranged? (**Note:** Three of the possible arrangements are *TOPS*, *TSPO*, and *STOP*.)

    A) 4          B) 6          C) 12         D) 24

*The end of the contest* ✍🏻 **5**

Solutions on Page 61 • Answers on Page 94

# 1990-91 Annual 5th Grade Contest

*Spring, 1991*

**5**

## Instructions

- **Time** You will have only *30 minutes* working time for this contest. You might be *unable* to finish all 30 questions in the time allowed.

- **Scores** Remember *this is a contest, not a test.* There is no "passing" or "failing" score. Few students score as high as 24 points (80% correct); students with even half that, 12 points, *deserve commendation!*

- **Format and Point Value** This is a multiple-choice contest. For each question, write the *capital letter* that is *in front of* the answer you choose. For each question, your answer will be one of the *capital letters* A, B, C, or D. Each question you answer correctly is worth 1 point. Unanswered questions receive no credit.

1. $1 \times 9 \times 9 \times 1 =$

   A) $1 \times 9$     B) $9 \times 9$     C) $1 \times 1$     D) $19 \times 19$

   1.

2. In the diagram shown at the right, line segment $AB$ is a diameter of the circle. If $AB = 10$, what is the length of a radius of the circle?

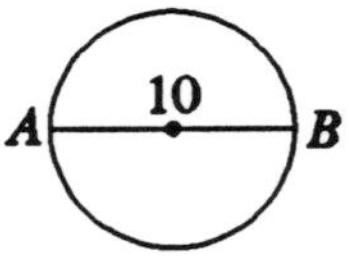

   A) 5     B) 10     C) 20     D) $10\pi$

   2.

3. $2 - 2 + 2 - 2 + 2 =$

   A) 10     B) 4     C) 2     D) 0

   3.

4. There are ten digits in our number system. What is the product of all *five* even digits?

   A) 384     B) 48     C) 32     D) 0

   4.

5. $11 \times 11 \times 11 =$

   A) 1111     B) 1221     C) 1331     D) 1441

   5.

6. $(4 - 1) \times (4 - 2) \times (4 - 3) \times (4 - 4) =$

   A) 0     B) 6     C) 24     D) 256

   6.

7. Find the missing number: $8 \times 8 = 16 \times \underline{?}$

   A) 16     B) 4     C) 2     D) 1

   7.

8. At Pete's Pizzeria, a pizza costs $6 and a soda costs 75¢. What is the total cost of 2 pizzas and 4 sodas (before taxes)?

   A) $13.50     B) $15.00     C) $25.50     D) $27.00

   8.

9. $9880 \div 8 =$

   A) 1234     B) 1235     C) 1236     D) 1237

   9.

10. Which of the following products is largest?

    A) $7 \times 13$     B) $8 \times 12$     C) $9 \times 11$     D) $10 \times 10$

    10.

11. $(1 \times 1) + (10 \times 10) + (100 \times 100) =$

    A) 111     B) 1001     C) 10101     D) 10201

    11.

*Go on to the next page* ⮕ **5**

| | | |
|---|---|---|
| 12. | The perimeter of the rectangle shown in the diagram is 20. The width of this rectangle is 4. What is the length of this rectangle? <br><br> 4 | 12. |
| | A) 5     B) 6     C) 16     D) 24 | |

12. The perimeter of the rectangle shown in the diagram is 20. The width of this rectangle is 4. What is the length of this rectangle?

    A) 5      B) 6      C) 16      D) 24

13. Find the missing number: $4321 = 1234 + \underline{\ ?\ }$

    A) 2222      B) 2345      C) 3087      D) 3187

14. What is the ones' digit in the product $987 \times 789$?

    A) 1      B) 3      C) 7      D) 9

15. $(111 + 111 + 111 + 111) - (11 + 11 + 11 + 11) =$

    A) 44      B) 400      C) 444      D) 1111

16. The number of sides of a square multiplied by the number of vertices of a square equals

    A) 8      B) 9      C) 12      D) 16

17. $(19 \times 91) - (19 \times 90) =$

    A) 19      B) 90      C) 1990      D) 1

18. How many seconds are there in 60 minutes?

    A) 1      B) 60      C) 3000      D) 3600

19. Find the missing number: $5 \times (3 + 4) = (5 \times 3) + \underline{\ ?\ }$

    A) 4      B) 12      C) 15      D) 20

20. Each angle in a rectangle is

    A) 90°      B) 60°      C) acute      D) obtuse

21. Mickey is twice as old as Donald and Donald is twice as old as Huey. If Huey is 12 years old, how old is Mickey?

    A) 3      B) 6      C) 24      D) 48

22. When a certain whole number is divided by 5, the remainder is odd. The original whole number *could be*

    A) 41      B) 47      C) 54      D) 59

*Go on to the next page* ⫸   **5**

23. I earn $5 an hour. If I work 5 hours a day for 5 days, what is the total amount of money I earn?

    A) $5      B) $25      C) $125      D) $555

    23.

24. When I divided a certain number by 3, the quotient was 663 and the remainder was 2. What was the original number?

    A) 666      B) 669      C) 1990      D) 1991

    24.

25. Five years ago my brother was 5 years younger than I was. If he is now 21 years old, how old will I be in 5 years?

    A) 16      B) 26      C) 31      D) 36

    25.

26. How many whole numbers greater than 9 and less than 999 are divisible by 9?

    A) 108      B) 109      C) 110      D) 111

    26.

27. Which of the following numbers leaves a remainder of 1 when divided by 2, 3, and 5?

    A) 31      B) 16      C) 11      D) 7

    27.

28. I have an equal number of pennies and nickels and no other coins. Which of the following *could be* the amount of money I have?

    A) 24¢      B) 25¢      C) 26¢      D) 27¢

    28.

29. If $2 + 4 + 6 + \ldots + 196 + 198 + 200 = 10\,100$, what is the value of $1 + 2 + 3 + \ldots + 98 + 99 + 100$?

    A) 1000      B) 5000      C) 5050      D) 10000

    29.

30. How many different rectangles does this diagram contain? (Count *all* the rectangles, no matter what size they are.)

    A) 4      B) 5      C) 9      D) 10

    30.

*The end of the contest* ✍    **5**

Solutions on Page 65 • Answers on Page 95

# 1986-87 Annual 6th Grade Contest

*Tuesday, March 3, 1987*

**6**

## Instructions

- **Time** You will have only *30 minutes* working time for this contest. You might be *unable* to finish all 40 questions in the time allowed.

- **Scores** Remember *this is a contest, not a test.* There is no "passing" or "failing" score. Few students score as high as 30 points (75% correct); students with even half that, 15 points, *deserve commendation!*

- **Format and Point Value** This is a multiple-choice contest. For each question, write the *capital letter* that is *in front of* the answer you choose. For each question, your answer will be one of the *capital letters* A, B, C, or D. Each question you answer correctly is worth 1 point. Unanswered questions receive no credit.

| | | Answers |
|---|---|---|
| 1. | 83 + 83 + 83 + 17 + 17 + 17 + 17 =<br>A) 300  B) 317  C) 383  D) 400 | 1. |
| 2. | If the average of two numbers is 7, the numbers could be<br>A) 3 and 4  B) 1 and 8  C) 2 and 14  D) 6 and 8 | 2. |
| 3. | Which of the following is an even number?<br>A) 666 + 777  B) 666 − 555  C) 666 × 333  D) 666 ÷ 222 | 3. |
| 4. | $(0 \times 1) + (0 \times 2) + (0 \times 3) + (0 \times 4) =$<br>A) 0  B) 10  C) 24  D) 25 | 4. |
| 5. | Find the degree-measure of one angle of a square.<br>A) 4°  B) 90°  C) 100°  D) 360° | 5. |
| 6. | 88888 − 9999 =<br>A) 11111  B) 78889  C) 77889  D) 79999 | 6. |
| 7. | The product of two whole numbers is 66. The largest that one of these numbers could possibly be is<br>A) 11  B) 22  C) 33  D) 66 | 7. |
| 8. | Find the missing number: $14 \times 15 \times 16 = 28 \times 30 \times \underline{\ ?\ }$<br>A) 2  B) 4  C) 8  D) 32 | 8. |
| 9. | Round 5499 to the nearest thousand.<br>A) 5000  B) 5400  C) 5500  D) 6000 | 9. |
| 10. | $1^1 + 1^2 + 1^3 + 1^4 =$<br>A) 4  B) 10  C) 14  D) 50 | 10. |
| 11. | From $3 \times 5 \times 7$, subtract $3 \times 5$. The result is<br>A) 7  B) $3 \times 5 \times 1$  C) $3 \times 5 \times 6$  D) $3 \times 5 \times 7$ | 11. |
| 12. | What per cent of the value of a quarter is the value of a dime?<br>A) 2/5%  B) 10%  C) 40%  D) 250% | 12. |
| 13. | $(5 \times 10) + (7 \times 1) + (4 \times 1000) + (3 \times 100) =$<br>A) 5743  B) 3457  C) 4357  D) 4537 | 13. |
| 14. | Jill is now 14 years old. Jack is now 6 years older than Jill was 2 years ago. How old is Jack now?<br>A) 10  B) 18  C) 20  D) 22 | 14. |
| 15. | The average of 99, 97, 95, 93, and 91 is<br>A) 95  B) 94  C) 95.5  D) 94.5 | 15. |

*Go on to the next page* |||||➡ **6**

| | |
|---|---|
| 16. In the diagram, there is an equilateral triangle and a square. If the perimeter of the triangle is 24, find the perimeter of the square. <br> A) 24     B) 32     C) 40     D) 96 | 16. |
| 17. 294 equals each of the following *except* <br> A) $(1\times100) + (19\times10) + 4$    B) $(1\times100) + (9\times10) + 104$ <br> C) $(2\times100) + (9\times10) + 4$    D) $(2\times100) + (9\times10) + 14$ | 17. |
| 18. How many whole numbers are greater than 777 and less than 888 <br> A) 100    B) 109    C) 110    D) 111 | 18. |
| 19. 11 is a factor of <br> A) 1    B) 111    C) 11 111    D) 111 111 | 19. |
| 20. 290 days is most nearly equal to <br> A) 288 days   B) 41 weeks   C) 9 months   D) 1 year | 20. |
| 21. $5 \times 2 \times 5 \times 2 \times 5 \times 2 \times 5 \times 2 \times 5 \times 2 =$ <br> A) 50    B) 10 000    C) 50 000    D) 100 000 | 21. |
| 22. Half the sum of two numbers is 20. If one of the numbers is 7, the other number is <br> A) 3    B) 13    C) 26    D) 33 | 22. |
| 23. A boy has 100 nickels, 100 dimes, and 100 quarters. He has <br> A) $34    B) $39    C) $40    D) $75 | 23. |
| 24. $1\frac{1}{5} + 2\frac{2}{5} + 3\frac{3}{5} + 4\frac{4}{5} =$ <br> A) 6    B) 10    C) 12    D) 13 | 24. |
| 25. I was paid $1 on the first day, and my salary doubled each day thereafter. In total, how much did I earn in the first 7 days? <br> A) $63    B) $64    C) $127    D) $128 | 25. |
| 26. Find the ones' digit of the difference $7^2 - 6^2$. <br> A) 4    B) 3    C) 2    D) 1 | 26. |
| 27. $10 - 9 + 9 - 8 + 8 - 7 + 7 - 6 + 6 - 5 + 5 - 4 + 4 - 3 + 3 =$ <br> A) 10    B) 7    C) 1    D) 0 | 27. |
| 28. When 1 is divided by $\frac{1}{2}$, the quotient is <br> A) $\frac{1}{2}$    B) 1    C) $1\frac{1}{2}$    D) 2 | 28. |
| 29. The square root of the square root of 16 is <br> A) 2    B) 4    C) 16    D) 64 | 29. |

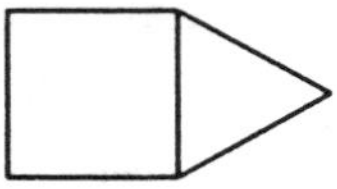

*Go on to the next page* ⮕ **6**

| | |
|---|---|
| 30. Which of the following is divisible by 2, 3, 4, and 5?<br>    A) 2001        B) 2010        C) 2100        D) 2110 | 30. |
| 31. Al, Bob, and Carl together spent $24, of which half was spent by Al and one-third was spent by Bob. How much did Carl spend?<br>    A) $4        B) $6        C) $8        D) $20 | 31. |
| 32. The perimeter of a square is 4. The area of the square is<br>    A) 1        B) 2        C) 4        D) 16 | 32. |
| 33. Find the largest *prime* factor of 30 × 40 × 50.<br>    A) 3        B) 5        C) 10        D) 50 | 33. |
| 34. Increasing $100 by a certain percent produces the same result as decreasing $300 by the same percent. This percent is<br>    A) 200%        B) 150%        C) 100%        D) 50% | 34. |
| 35. In the correct addition at the right, $A$, $B$, and $C$ are 3 different non-zero digits. Find the value of $C$.    $\begin{array}{r} A\,B \\ +\,C\,C \\ \hline A\,A\,A \end{array}$  $B+C=A$  $A+C=A$<br>    A) 1        B) 9        C) 8        D) 7 | 35. |
| 36. Think of the largest whole number less than 10 000 whose digits are all different. What is the ones' digit of this number?<br>    A) 6        B) 7        C) 8        D) 9 | 36. |
| 37. If 3 tics = 4 tacs, and 2 tacs = 3 toes, then 1 toe =<br>    A) $\frac{1}{6}$ tic        B) $\frac{1}{2}$ tic        C) 2 tics        D) 6 tics | 37. |
| 38. When the last 3 digits of a year (such as 1987) are consecutive digits written in descending order, we'll call the year a *descending* year. A *descending* year will next occur in the<br>    A) 23rd century        B) 24th century<br>    C) 25th century        D) 26th century | 38. |
| 39. A circle has an area of $36\pi$. What is the area of the smallest square that can surround this circle?<br>    A) 18        B) 36        C) 72        D) 144 | 39. |
| 40. All the whole numbers with a first digit of 2 are written in increasing order. The list begins 2, 20, 21, 22, . . . . Find the *1000th digit* thus written.<br>    A) 6        B) 7        C) 8        D) 9 | 40. |

*The end of the contest* ✍️  **6**

Solutions on Page 69 • Answers on Page 96

# 1987-88 Annual 6th Grade Contest

*Tuesday, March 8, 1988*

**6**

## Instructions

- **Time** You will have only *30 minutes* working time for this contest. You might be *unable* to finish all 40 questions in the time allowed.

- **Scores** Remember *this is a contest, not a test*. There is no "passing" or "failing" score. Few students score as high as 30 points (75% correct); students with even half that, 15 points, *deserve commendation!*

- **Format and Point Value** This is a multiple-choice contest. For each question, write the *capital letter* that is *in front of* the answer you choose. For each question, your answer will be one of the *capital letters* A, B, C, or D. Each question you answer correctly is worth 1 point. Unanswered questions receive no credit.

Copyright © 1988 by Mathematics Leagues Inc.

| | |
|---|---|
| 1. Captain Quirk invited 26 Vulcons and 45 Clingons to visit the Interprise. How many more Clingons than Vulcons were invited?<br>A) 9     B) 11     C) 19     D) 29 | 1. |
| 2. $1492 + 1988 + 2001 =$<br>A) 5371     B) 5471     C) 5481     D) 5491 | 2. |
| 3. $20 \div (10 + 10) =$<br>A) 1     B) 2     C) 10     D) 12 | 3. |
| 4. $9 + 99 + 999 =$<br>A) 1007     B) 1087     C) 1097     D) 1107 | 4. |
| 5. The tens' digit of 1988 is less than its _?_ digit.<br>A) ones'     B) hundreds'     C) thousands'     D) ten-thousands' | 5. |
| 6. $99 \times 78 =$<br>A) 7612     B) 7622     C) 7712     D) 7722 | 6. |
| 7. If Al fished every day from July 17 through July 31, he fished<br>A) for 14 days   B) for 15 days   C) for 16 days   D) for 24 days | 7. |
| 8. $19 \times 88$ has the same value as $38 \times$ _?_<br>A) 44     B) 69     C) 88     D) 176 | 8. |
| 9. If the time now is 11:45 A.M., 59 minutes from now it will be<br>A) 10:46 A.M.   B) 12:44 A.M.   C) 12:44 P.M.   D) 12:46 P.M. | 9. |
| 10. For which of the following pairs of numbers is the product 1 more than the sum?<br>A) 1, 2     B) 2, 3     C) 3, 4     D) 4, 5 | 10. |
| 11.     $1 + 2 + 3 + 4 + 5 + 6 + 7 + 8 + 9$<br>$+ 1 + 2 + 3 + 4 + 5 + 6 + 7 + 8 + 9$<br>$+ 1 + 2 + 3 + 4 + 5 + 6 + 7 + 8 + 9$<br>$+ 1 + 2 + 3 + 4 + 5 + 6 + 7 + 8 + 9 =$<br>A) 45     B) 49     C) 180     D) 445 | 11. |
| 12. The sum of two prime numbers is always<br>A) even                 B) odd<br>C) divisible by 3     D) greater than 3 | 12. |
| 13. $10 + 10 + 10 + 10 + 10 + 10 + 10 + 10 + 10 + 10 =$<br>A) $10^2$     B) $10^{10}$     C) $10^{100}$     D) $10^{1000}$ | 13. |
| 14. The sum of five hundred nine and three hundred twenty-eight is<br>A) 387     B) 827     C) 837     D) 917 | 14. |
| 15. The year "1988" contains two equal digits. Of the years from 1988 through 2001, how many have *three* equal digits?<br>A) 1     B) 2     C) 10     D) 11 | 15. |
| 16. Which of the following numbers is divisible by 15?<br>A) 225     B) 425     C) 515     D) 1550 | 16. |

17. The prime numbers 7 and 17 both contain the digit 7. The next | 17.
    prime which contains the digit 7 is
    A) 27          B) 37          C) 47          D) 57

18. The sum of four whole numbers is always | 18.
    A) even                        B) odd
    C) a whole number              D) divisible by 4

19. In the diagram at the right, | 19.
    the ratio of shaded circles
    to all circles is
    A) 1:2          B) 1:1          C) 2:1          D) 6:11

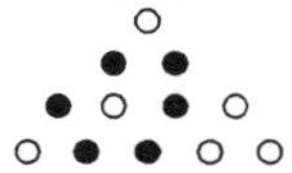

20. The average of two numbers is 8 and their product is 55. The | 20.
    larger of the two numbers is
    A) 5          B) 7          C) 9          D) 11

21. Round 999 999 to the nearest ten. | 21.
    A) 999 900      B) 999 990      C) 999 000      D) 1 000 000

22. Which of the following is between $10^3$ and $10^4$? | 22.
    A) $2^5$          B) $2^6$          C) $2^9$          D) $2^{13}$

23. The product of two consecutive integers is 2550. The larger of | 23.
    these two integers is
    A) 25          B) 26          C) 50          D) 51

24. The difference between the measure of one angle of a square | 24.
    and the measure of one angle of an equilateral triangle is
    A) 30°          B) 45°          C) 60°          D) 90°

25. If 1 bleep = 6 peeps, then 600 peeps = | 25.
    A) 10 bleeps    B) 100 bleeps    C) 3600 bleeps    D) 6000 bleeps

26. $26^3 - 25^3 =$ | 26.
    A) 1          B) 1951          C) 1973          D) 1987

27. Postcards are sold in packages of 250. If Joy wants 4500 post- | 27.
    cards, then she should buy _?_ packages.
    A) 9          B) 16          C) 18          D) 20

28. $\frac{2}{3} + \frac{2}{3} + \frac{2}{3} =$ | 28.

    A) 1          B) $1\frac{1}{3}$          C) $1\frac{2}{3}$          D) 2

29. Red pens are sold at 3 for $1 and black pens are sold at 4 for | 29.
    $1.50. Alice bought 12 red pens and 24 black pens. She paid
    for them with a $20 bill. How much change did she receive?
    A) $7          B) $9          C) $13          D) $16

30. The length of each side of a square is a whole number of cm. | 30.
    Which of the following could be the area of the square?
    A) 200 cm$^2$      B) 300 cm$^2$      C) 400 cm$^2$      D) 500 cm$^2$

| | | |
|---|---|---|
| 31. | 365 days from March 2, 1988 is __?__ , 1989.<br>A) March 1    B) March 2    C) March 3    D) March 4 | 31. |
| 32. | In the diagram at the right<br>$AB = 20$ and $BC = 15$. Find<br>the perimeter of *ABCDEF*.<br><br>A) 35    B) 70    C) 75    D) 80 | 32. |
| 33. | From the first 25 positive whole numbers, 5 numbers, all even, are removed. What per cent of the remaining numbers are even?<br>A) 20%    B) 25%    C) 28%    D) 35% | 33. |
| 34. | On a 20-question test, correct answers are worth 5 points, un-answered questions are worth 2 points, and incorrect answers are worth 0 points. If Steve answered 10 questions and got 5 correct, his score was<br>A) 25    B) 45    C) 50    D) 55 | 34. |
| 35. | The symbol ☐ , drawn any size, means "square the number in-side." For example, ⑤ , means 5 × 5, or 25. The value of ④ is<br>A) 256    B) 128    C) 64    D) 516 | 35. |
| 36. | If the pattern of the first 4 letters of *ABCDABCDABCD* . . . con-tinues to the right, the 1988th letter in the pattern would be<br>A) *A*    B) *B*    C) *C*    D) *D* | 36. |
| 37. | The sum of the areas of the two congruent circles shown is $72\pi$. The area of rectangle *ABCD* is<br>A) 72    B) 144    C) 288    D) 576 | 37. |
| 38. | Four different whole numbers between 10 and 99 are multipli-ed together. Which of the following could be their product?<br>A) 6561    B) 10 001    C) 28 101 810   D) 99 999 999 | 38. |
| 39. | Two cars are traveling in the same direction, one at 40 km/hr and the other at 50 km/hr. If the slower car is 15 km ahead of the faster car, how long will it take the faster car to catch up with the slower car?<br>A) 60 minutes   B) 75 minutes   C) 80 minutes   D) 90 minutes | 39. |
| 40. | The number 1000 has only 16 positive whole number factors. The product of all 16 of these factors is<br>A) $10^8$    B) $10^{16}$    C) $10^{24}$    D) $10^{32}$ | 40. |

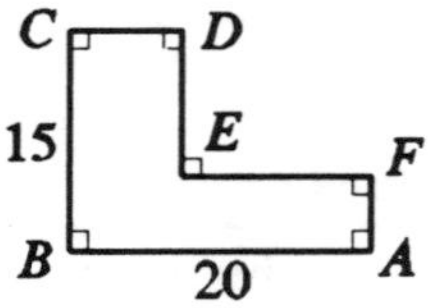

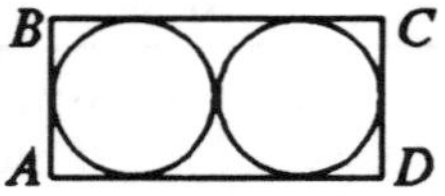

*The end of the contest* ✍ **6**

Solutions on Page 73 • Answers on Page 97

# 1988-89 Annual 6th Grade Contest

*Tuesday, March 14, 1989*

**6**

## Instructions

- **Time** You will have only *30 minutes* working time for this contest. You might be *unable* to finish all 40 questions in the time allowed.

- **Scores** Remember *this is a contest, not a test.* There is no "passing" or "failing" score. Few students score as high as 30 points (75% correct); students with even half that, 15 points, *deserve commendation!*

- **Format and Point Value** This is a multiple-choice contest. For each question, write the *capital letter* that is *in front of* the answer you choose. For each question, your answer will be one of the *capital letters* A, B, C, or D. Each question you answer correctly is worth 1 point. Unanswered questions receive no credit.

| | | Answers |
|---|---|---|
| 1. | $(1 \times 9 \times 8 \times 9) \div (9 \times 8 \times 9 \times 1) =$ <br> A) 0      B) 1      C) 2      D) 1989 | 1. |
| 2. | An insect collector caught 123 mayflies in May, 234 Junebugs in June, and 345 fireflies in July. During this time, he caught <br> A) 456 insects   B) 678 insects   C) 602 insects   D) 702 insects | 2. |
| 3. | $3223 - 1989 =$ <br> A) 2234      B) 1324      C) 1234      D) 1144 | 3. |
| 4. | How many seconds are there in 6 minutes? <br> A) 10      B) 36      C) 60      D) 360 | 4. |
| 5. | Find the missing number: $100 \times 99 \times 100 = 9900 \times$ _?_ <br> A) 10      B) 100      C) 1000      D) 9900 | 5. |
| 6. | Which has the greatest product? <br> A) $1 \times 9 \times 8 \times 7$   B) $1 \times 9 \times 8 \times 8$   C) $1 \times 9 \times 8 \times 9$   D) $1 \times 9 \times 9 \times 0$ | 6. |
| 7. | $10\ 101 + 99\ 999 =$ <br> A) 19 191      B) 101 010      C) 110 100      D) 119 191 | 7. |
| 8. | The least common multiple of 18 and 30 is <br> A) 90      B) 18      C) 12      D) 6 | 8. |
| 9. | $(123 \times 456) - (123 \times 455) =$ <br> A) 456      B) 455      C) 123      D) 1 | 9. |
| 10. | Round 9.898 to the nearest hundredth. <br> A) 9.89      B) 9.90      C) 9.99      D) 10.00 | 10. |
| 11. | Of the following, which is the largest factor of $2 \times 4 \times 5 \times 6$? <br> A) 4      B) 6      C) 8      D) 16 | 11. |
| 12. | How much greater is the tens' digit of 1989 than the hundreds' digit of 1492? <br> A) 1      B) 4      C) 5      D) 6 | 12. |
| 13. | $48 + 49 + 50 + 51 + 52 = 46 + 47 +$ _?_ $+ 53 + 54.$ <br> A) 0      B) 4      C) 46      D) 50 | 13. |
| 14. | If the area of the shaded region of the square is 24, the area of the entire square is <br> A) 8      B) 32      C) 48      D) 96 | 14. |
| 15. | Mickey Moose and Ronald Duck ate 6 sandwiches between them. If Mickey ate twice as many sandwiches as Ronald, how many sandwiches did Ronald eat? <br> A) 4      B) 3      C) 2      D) 1 | 15. |

*Go on to the next page* ⟾ **6**

| | | |
|---|---|---|
| 16. | The sum of one million and one thousand is<br>A) 1 001 000   B) 1 000 100   C) 101 000   D) 100 100 | 16. |
| 17. | The sum of the first 5 positive prime numbers is<br>A) 28   B) 26   C) 18   D) 17 | 17. |
| 18. | Mike Tyson earned about $22 000 000 for a fight that lasted 91 seconds. In this fight, his earnings per second was closest to<br>A) $2 400   B) $24 000   C) $240 000   D) $2 400 000 | 18. |
| 19. | What is the sum of all the whole number factors less than 28 that are factors of 28?<br>A) 11   B) 12   C) 14   D) 28 | 19. |
| 20. | Last year, I paid 60¢ each week for *TV Guide*. How much (to the nearest $10) did I spend for *TV Guide* last year?<br>A) $300   B) $60   C) $30   D) $10 | 20. |
| 21. | $(247 \times 1000) + (247 \times 100) + (247 \times 10) + (247 \times 1)$ is divisible by<br>A) 2   B) 3   C) 4   D) 11 | 21. |
| 22. | The square of the perimeter of a square is 400. The area of the square is<br>A) 5   B) 25   C) 100   D) 400 | 22. |
| 23. | It takes 2000 bees 1 year to make 7 jars of honey. How long will it take 5000 bees to make 70 jars of honey?<br>A) 2 years   B) 4 years   C) 5 years   D) 7 years | 23. |
| 24. | $2 + 2 + 2 + 2 + 2 + 2 + 2 + 2 =$<br>A) $2^3$   B) $2^4$   C) $2^8$   D) $2^{16}$ | 24. |
| 25. | In the diagram, the semicircle shown has a diameter of 10. What is the perimeter of this entire region?<br>A) $5\pi$   B) $10\pi$   C) $5\pi + 10$   D) $10\pi + 10$ | 25. |
| 26. | Find the missing number in the following equation:<br>$(3 \times 4 \times 5) + (3 \times 4 \times 6) = (3 \times 4 \times 10) + (3 \times 4 \times \underline{?})$.<br>A) 1   B) 3   C) 20   D) 21 | 26. |
| 27. | One angle of an isosceles triangle has a measure of 120°. Another angle of this triangle must have a measure of<br>A) 20°   B) 30°   C) 40°   D) 60° | 27. |
| 28. | In an Olympic event, the winner of a triathlon swam for 1 hour 42 minutes, then biked for 6 hours 59 minutes, then ran for 6 hours 13 minutes. If he started at 9:00 A.M., he finished at<br>A) 10:54 P.M.   B) 11:54 P.M.   C) 12:54 P.M.   D) 1:54 A.M. | 28. |
| 29. | A certain whole number greater than 1 is divisible only by 1 and itself. This number is always<br>A) even   B) odd   C) a square   D) a prime | 29. |

| | | |
|---|---|---|
| 30. | At the end of each day, my bank adds $3 to my bank account for every dollar in my account. I began with $1 and never touched my account. At the end of 3 days, how much money was in this account?<br><br>A) $27      B) $28      C) $49      D) $64 | 30. |
| 31. | At 4 o'clock, a pole 10 m high casts a shadow 15 m long. At the same time, how long is a shadow cast by a pole 6 m high?<br>A) 11 m      B) 10 m      C) 9 m      D) 8 m | 31. |
| 32. | A bike's front wheel has twice the radius of its rear wheel. In riding, when the front wheel turns twice, the rear wheel turns<br>A) once      B) twice      C) 4 times      D) 8 times | 32. |
| 33. | The average of 21 consecutive integers is 31. The largest of these integers must be<br><br>A) 40      B) 41      C) 51      D) 52 | 33. |
| 34. | An integer is divisible by 5, 6, 8, and 9. This integer must always also be divisible by<br>A) 28      B) 360      C) 720      D) 5689 | 34. |
| 35. | The larger square shown at the right has an area of 100. The vertices of the other square lie at the midpoints of the sides of the larger square. The area of the smaller square shown must be<br>A) 80      B) 75      C) 50      D) 10 | 35. |
| 36. | A 1200-word story averaged 5 letters per word and had a vowel to consonant ratio of 3:5. This story contained _?_ consonants.<br>A) 2250      B) 3600      C) 3750      D) 10 000 | 36. |
| 37. | A cat runs 3 times as fast as a mouse. If a mouse runs at 2 m per second and is 12 m from a cat, the mouse will be caught in<br>A) 2 seconds    B) 3 seconds    C) 4 seconds    D) 6 seconds | 37. |
| 38. | In the 4 by 5 rectangle shown, there are 14 dots on the outside. If I drew a 1988 by 1989 rectangle made up of dots (as in the diagram), how many dots would there be on the outside?<br>A) 7950      B) 7952      C) 7954      D) 7956 | 38. |
| 39. | If the pattern of the first 4 letters of *MATHMATHMATH* . . . continues to the right, the 1989th letter would be<br>A) *A*      B) *T*      C) *H*      D) *M* | 39. |
| 40. | If I add the 1 million whole numbers from 1 to 1 million, then my ones' digit will be<br>A) 0      B) 1      C) 5      D) 9 | 40. |

*The end of the contest*   **6**

Solutions on Page 77 • Answers on Page 98

# 1989-90 Annual 6th Grade Contest

*Tuesday, March 13, 1990*

**6**

## Instructions

- **Time** You will have only *30 minutes* working time for this contest. You might be *unable* to finish all 40 questions in the time allowed.

- **Scores** Remember *this is a contest, not a test.* There is no "passing" or "failing" score. Few students score as high as 30 points (75% correct); students with even half that, 15 points, *deserve commendation!*

- **Format and Point Value** This is a multiple-choice contest. For each question, write the *capital letter* that is *in front of* the answer you choose. For each question, your answer will be one of the *capital letters* A, B, C, or D. Each question you answer correctly is worth 1 point. Unanswered questions receive no credit.

| | | | | | Answers |
|---|---|---|---|---|---|

1. $(1 + 9) \times (9 + 0) =$

    A) 0        B) 10        C) 90        D) 1990
    1.

2. 20 nickels have the same value as

    A) 5 dimes     B) 100 pennies   C) 5 quarters   D) 2 dollars
    2.

3. $9898 - 8989 =$

    A) 89        B) 909       C) 989       D) 1010
    3.

4. Catman pays 25¢ every 20 minutes to park his Catmobile. If Catman has $1, for how long can Catman park?

    A) 4 minutes   B) 5 minutes    C) 60 minutes  D) 80 minutes
    4.

5. $\sqrt{113}$ is between

    A) 9 and 10    B) 10 and 11   C) 56 and 57   D) 112 and 114
    5.

6. In the word *mathematics*, the ratio of the number of letters that are vowels to the number that are consonants is

    A) 4:7        B) 7:4       C) 4:11      D) 7:11
    6.

7. $7 \div 7 \times 7 =$

    A) 0        B) $1 \div 7$    C) 1        D) 7
    7.

8. $1\ m - 1\ cm =$

    A) 99 cm    B) 9 cm     C) 99 m     D) 9 m
    8.

9. $(1 \times 10^3) + (9 \times 10^2) + (9 \times 10^1) =$

    A) 199       B) 1990     C) 19900    D) 81000
    9.

10. An even prime number is subtracted from an odd prime number. If the result is 1, the odd prime number must be

    A) 1        B) 2       C) 3       D) 5
    10.

11. $(20 \times 20 \times 20) \div (40 \times 40 \times 40) =$

    A) 0.125    B) 0.25    C) 0.5     D) 2
    11.

12. 4 hours 55 mins. + 2 hours 48 mins. = ? hours ? mins.

    A) 2, 7     B) 7, 3     C) 7, 33    D) 7, 43
    12.

13. Find the missing number: $13+14+15+16+17 = 15 \times ?$

    A) 3        B) 5       C) 15      D) 17
    13.

14. A triangle can intersect a circle in at most

    A) 6 points   B) 5 points   C) 4 points   D) 3 points
    14.

15. Today is Tuesday. In 31 days, it will be a

    A) Tuesday   B) Wednesday   C) Thursday   D) Friday
    15.

*Go on to the next page* ⟫ **6**

| | |
|---|---|
| 16. How many positive whole number factors does 16 have?<br>A) 2     B) 4     C) 5     D) 8 | 16. |
| 17. On this 40-question contest, if I answer exactly 10 questions *correctly*, what percent of the 40 questions would I get *wrong*?<br>A) 25%     B) 30%     C) 40%     D) 75% | 17. |
| 18. $256 - 128 =$<br>A) $2^5$     B) $2^6$     C) $2^7$     D) $2^8$ | 18. |
| 19. If two numbers have a sum of 12 and a difference of 2, what is the product of the two numbers?<br>A) 35     B) 24     C) 14     D) 6 | 19. |
| 20. My tickets are consecutively numbered from 19 to 90. I have<br>A) 70 tickets    B) 71 tickets    C) 72 tickets    D) 109 tickets | 20. |
| 21. If the pendulum of a very big clock completes one swing in 2 seconds, how many swings will it complete in 1 hour?<br>A) 30     B) 1800     C) 3600     D) 7200 | 21. |
| 22. Find the missing number: $10 \times 20 \times 30 = 1000 \times$ ?<br>A) 6     B) 60     C) 600     D) 6000 | 22. |
| 23. Of the following numbers, which is the largest?<br>A) $1^4$     B) $2^3$     C) $3^2$     D) $4^1$ | 23. |
| 24. What is the area of a square whose perimeter is 48?<br>A) 192     B) 144     C) 48     D) 36 | 24. |
| 25. I get a penny the 1st day and a nickel the 2nd. If this alternating pattern continues, how much will I have in 20 days?<br>A) 20¢     B) 30¢     C) 60¢     D) $1.20 | 25. |
| 26. $(7+8+9) - 7 + (7+8+9) - 8 + (7+8+9) - 9 =$<br>A) $1 \times (7+8+9)$   B) $2 \times (7+8+9)$   C) $3 \times (7+8+9)$   D) $4 \times (7+8+9)$ | 26. |
| 27. The sides of a triangle could have lengths 10, 4, and<br>A) 1     B) 4     C) 6     D) 13 | 27. |
| 28. John won $400, gave 40% to his brother, and spent 10% of the *remainder*. How much money did John have left?<br>A) $200     B) $216     C) $240     D) $350 | 28. |
| 29. In a certain triangle, the largest angle equals the sum of the other two angles. The measure of the largest angle is<br>A) 30°     B) 45°     C) 60°     D) 90° | 29. |

*Go on to the next page* ⟩⟩⟩ **6**

30. I bought 6 tapes for $1 each and 8 more tapes for $15 each. What was my average cost per tape for these 14 tapes?

    A) $7.50    B) $8.00    C) $9.00    D) $12.00

30.

31. The product of two prime numbers *cannot* be

    A) positive    B) odd    C) even    D) prime

31.

32. What is the circumference of a circle whose area is $\pi$?

    A) 1    B) $\pi$    C) $2\pi$    D) $4\pi$

32.

33. $10 \times 10 \times 10 \times 10 \times 10 \times 10 \times 10 \times 10 \times 10 \times 10 =$

    A) $100^5$    B) $1000^4$    C) $10000^3$    D) 1 million

33.

34. The thousands' digit of $1 \times 2 \times 3 \times \ldots \times 19 \times 20$ is

    A) 0    B) 1    C) 2    D) 5

34.

35. My bicycle has a rear wheel whose diameter is 1.2 times as big as the diameter of the front wheel. As I ride my bicycle, if the front wheel turns 120 times, the rear wheel will turn

    A) 96 times    B) 100 times    C) 120 times    D) 144 times

35.

36. The time 1.9 hours past 12:04 P.M. is

    A) 1:13 P.M.    B) 1:54 P.M.    C) 1:58 P.M.    D) 2:00 P.M.

36.

37. How many whole numbers less than 50 can be written as the product of two or more consecutive whole numbers?

    A) 25    B) 8    C) 7    D) 6

37.

38. If the radius of the circle is 6, the total of the areas of all the shaded regions is

    A) $6\pi$    B) $12\pi$    C) $18\pi$    D) $36\pi$

38.

39. How many whole numbers between 100 and 1000 have the digit 1 in the tens' column?

    A) 89    B) 90    C) 99    D) 100

39.

40. From the first 20 positive whole numbers, 5 odd numbers are removed. The sum of the remaining 15 numbers *could* be

    A) 163    B) 168    C) 186    D) 196

40.

*The end of the contest* ✍ **6**

Solutions on Page 81 • Answers on Page 99

# 1990-91 Annual 6th Grade Contest

*Tuesday, March 12, 1991*

**6**

## Instructions

- **Time** You will have only *30 minutes* working time for this contest. You might be *unable* to finish all 40 questions in the time allowed.

- **Scores** Remember *this is a contest, not a test.* There is no "passing" or "failing" score. Few students score as high as 30 points (75% correct); students with even half that, 15 points, *deserve commendation!*

- **Format and Point Value** This is a multiple-choice contest. For each question, write the *capital letter* that is *in front of* the answer you choose. For each question, your answer will be one of the *capital letters* A, B, C, or D. Each question you answer correctly is worth 1 point. Unanswered questions receive no credit.

Copyright © 1991 by Mathematics Leagues Inc.

| | | | |
|---|---|---|---|
| 1. | $(1 + 1) \times (1 + 1) \times (1 + 1) =$ <br> A) 8     B) 6     C) 4     D) 1 | | 1. |
| 2. | If I eat 3 meals each day, how many meals do I eat each week? <br> A) 3     B) 7     C) 15     D) 21 | | 2. |
| 3. | $11 + 22 + 33 + 44 =$ <br> A) 90     B) 100     C) 109     D) 110 | | 3. |
| 4. | Two numbers have a sum of 4 and a difference of 4. What is the product of the two numbers? <br> A) 0     B) 4     C) 8     D) 16 | | 4. |
| 5. | $(1 \div 1) + (2 \div 2) + (3 \div 3) =$ <br> A) 1     B) 3     C) 4     D) 6 | | 5. |
| 6. | Which of the following is an odd number when simplified? <br> A) $4 + 4$     B) $4 - 4$     C) $4 \times 4$     D) $4 \div 4$ | | 6. |
| 7. | $1 \times 11 \times 111 =$ <br> A) 1111     B) 1221     C) 1331     D) 1441 | | 7. |
| 8. | What is the greatest common factor of 24 and 42? <br> A) 6     B) 8     C) 12     D) 24 | | 8. |
| 9. | The sum of the four whole number factors of 6 equals <br> A) $1 \times 6$     B) $2 \times 6$     C) $3 \times 6$     D) $4 \times 6$ | | 9. |
| 10. | The square of a certain whole number is greater than 36 and less than 64. The whole number is <br> A) 5     B) 6     C) 7     D) 8 | | 10. |
| 11. | 1991 divided by 11 equals <br> A) 161     B) 171     C) 181     D) 191 | | 11. |
| 12. | Of the following, which is the largest number? <br> A) $2 \times 2 \times 2 \times 2$   B) $3 \times 3 \times 3$   C) $4 \times 4$   D) $2 \times 3 \times 4$ | | 12. |
| 13. | Add the number of *even* integers both greater than 0 and less than 1000 to the number of *odd* integers both greater than 0 and less than 1000. What is this sum? <br> A) 499     B) 500     C) 999     D) 1000 | | 13. |
| 14. | $144 =$ <br> A) $2^4 \times 3^2$     B) $2^5 \times 3^1$     C) $2^3 \times 3^3$     D) $2^2 \times 3^4$ | | 14. |
| 15. | $121212 \div 12 =$ <br> A) 111     B) 1001     C) 1212     D) 10101 | | 15. |

*Go on to the next page* ▓▶ **6**

16. What is the average of 1990, 1991, and 1992?
    A) 1991        B) 1992        C) 1993        D) 5973

    16.

17. In the diagram at the right, rectangle *ABCD*  $B \quad E \quad C$
    is divided into two squares by line segment
    *EF*. If the perimeter of each square is 24,
    what is the perimeter of rectangle *ABCD*?  $A \quad F \quad D$
    A) 36        B) 40        C) 48        D) 96

    17.

18. Find the missing number: 1111 = 1001 + ?
    A) 11        B) 110        C) 111        D) 1100

    18.

19. How many quarters are there in $25?
    A) 10        B) 25        C) 100        D) 500

    19.

20. $\sqrt{4} \times \sqrt{4} \times \sqrt{4} \times \sqrt{4} =$
    A) 4        B) 8        C) 16        D) 32

    20.

21. I am 10 years older than my brother. Ten years ago, he was 10.
    How old will I be in ten years?
    A) 10        B) 20        C) 30        D) 40

    21.

22. Find the missing number: $6^2 \times 10^2 = 4^2 \times$ ?
    A) $3^2$        B) $5^2$        C) $15^2$        D) $30^2$

    22.

23. 100% of 200% equals
    A) 20%        B) 200%        C) 2000%        D) 20000%

    23.

24. Of the following, which is nearest in value to 123×456?
    A) 4000        B) 5000        C) 40000        D) 50000

    24.

25. $(1 \times 2 \times 3 \times 4 \times 5) \div (1 + 2 + 3 + 4 + 5) =$
    A) 1        B) 5        C) 8        D) 12

    25.

26. The sum of two positive whole numbers is 10. What is the
    least possible value of the product of these two numbers?
    A) 0        B) 1        C) 9        D) 10

    26.

27. Points *A*, *B*, *C*, and *D* lie on a line,
    as shown in the diagram. If *AC* = 20,      $A \quad B\ C \quad D$
    *BD* = 15, and *AD* = 30, then *CD* =
    A) 5        B) 10        C) 15        D) 20

    27.

28. How many positive prime numbers are divisible by 13?
    A) 0        B) 1        C) 2        D) 13

    28.

29. If 14 days ago was a Tuesday, what day will it be 14 days from
    today?
    A) Tuesday        B) Wednesday        C) Thursday        D) Friday

    29.

| | |
|---|---|
| 30. | Which of the following numbers is divisible by 9? <br> A) 333      B) 444      C) 777      D) 888 | 30. |

30. Which of the following numbers is divisible by 9?
    A) 333      B) 444      C) 777      D) 888

**30.**

31. $10 \times 100 \times 1000 =$
    A) $10^6$      B) $10^7$      C) $10^8$      D) $10^9$

**31.**

32. What is the remainder when 9876 is divided by 6789?
    A) 0      B) 1      C) 1111      D) 3087

**32.**

33. The product of two consecutive whole numbers is 9900. What is the sum of these two numbers?
    A) 19      B) 199      C) 1109      D) 9901

**33.**

34. I have twice as much money as my brother. If I have $10 more than he does, how much money do I have?
    A) $5      B) $10      C) $15      D) $20

**34.**

35. In the diagram at the right, the perimeter of the larger square is 36 and the perimeter of the smaller square is 16. What is the area of the shaded region?
    A) 4      B) 20      C) 25      D) 65

**35.**

36. There are exactly 15 prime numbers less than 50. Exactly how many prime numbers are less than 60?
    A) 19      B) 18      C) 17      D) 16

**36.**

37. When a certain positive number is rounded to the nearest hundred, the rounded number is twice as large as the original number. What is the original number?
    A) 25      B) 50      C) 100      D) 150

**37.**

38. The sum of nine of the first ten positive whole numbers is 50. Which of these ten whole numbers *didn't* I add?
    A) 1      B) 3      C) 5      D) 7

**38.**

39. $(2 + 4 + 6 + \ldots + 98 + 100) - (1 + 3 + 5 + \ldots + 97 + 99) =$
    A) 1      B) 49      C) 50      D) 100

**39.**

40. I have rectangular blocks that are 5 cm by 4 cm by 2 cm. What is the greatest number of these blocks that can fit in a box whose inner dimensions are 10 cm by 8 cm by 6 cm?
    A) 10      B) 12      C) 20      D) 60

**40.**

*The end of the contest* ✍ **6**

# Solutions

## 1988-89 Annual 4th Grade Contest
### Spring, 1989

**4**

### Contest Information

- **Solutions** Turn the page for detailed contest solutions (written in the question boxes) and letter answers (in the answer columns on the right).

- **Scores** When reviewing these questions, remember *this is a contest, not a test*. There is no "passing" or "failing" score. Few students score as high as 24 points (80% correct); students with even half that, 12 points, *deserve commendation!*

- **Answers & Rating Scale** Turn to page 90 for the letter answers to each question and the rating scale for this contest.

| | | | | | |
|---|---|---|---|---|---|
| 1. | 19 + 89 = 108, so the correct answer is choice C. | | | | 1. |
| | A) 1989 | B) 918 | C) 108 | D) 98 | C |
| 2. | The 26th letter is *z*; two letters before this is *x*. | | | | 2. |
| | A) *w* | B) *x* | C) *y* | D) *z* | B |
| 3. | (1 + 2 + 3 + 4 + 5)–(5 + 4 + 3 + 2 + 1) = 15–15 = 0. | | | | 3. |
| | A) 0 | B) 2 | C) 15 | D) 30 | A |
| 4. | 6 + 5 = 11; 6–5 = 1; 6 × 5 = 30; so choice D is correct. | | | | 4. |
| | A) 6 + 5 | B) 6–5 | C) 6 × 5 | D) 6 ÷ 5 | D |
| 5. | The product of 9 and 221 is 9 × 221 = 1989. | | | | 5. |
| | A) 230 | B) 1899 | C) 1989 | D) 1999 | C |
| 6. | (99 × 10) + (99 × 1) = 99 × (10 + 1) = 99 × 11 = 1089. | | | | 6. |
| | A) 209 | B) 999 | C) 1089 | D) 1099 | C |
| 7. | The number which is 3 more than 99 is 102. The number which is 2 less than 102 is 100. | | | | 7. C |
| | A) 94 | B) 98 | C) 100 | D) 104 | |
| 8. | 100 × 10 × 1 × 0 = 0, so choice D is correct. | | | | 8. |
| | A) 1110 | B) 1000 | C) 111 | D) 0 | D |
| 9. | When 1234 is divided by 56, the quotient is 22 and the remainder is 2. The sum of 22 and 2 is 24. | | | | 9. D |
| | A) 2 | B) 20 | C) 22 | D) 24 | |
| 10. | 121 × 121 = 14641. | | | | 10. |
| | A) 14641 | B) 484 | C) 242 | D) 121 | A |
| 11. | Since Pat's teacher is 26 years older than Pat and Pat is 9, Pat's teacher is 26 + 9 = 35. | | | | 11. B |
| | A) 34 | B) 35 | C) 36 | D) 37 | |

*Go on to the next page* ▐▶   **4**

| | |
|---|---|
| 12. $9 + 80 + 700 + 6000 = 6789$, so choice A is correct.<br><br>A) 6789        B) 6798        C) 9876        D) 30000 | 12.<br><br>A |
| 13. 1 hundred + 11 tens + 111 ones = $100 + 110 + 111 = 321$.<br><br>A) 123        B) 222        C) 321        D) 1221 | 13.<br><br>C |
| 14. $3000 \div 30 = 100$, so choice B is correct.<br><br>A) 10        B) 100        C) 300        D) 1000 | 14.<br><br>B |
| 15. The product *must* be divisible by 16. Since 0, 48, and 80 are all divisible by 16 while 72 is *not*, the correct answer is choice C.<br><br>A) 0        B) 48        C) 72        D) 80 | 15.<br><br>C |
| 16. $(50 \times 30) + (50 \times 9) + (1 \times 30) + (1 \times 9) = (50 \times 39) + (1 \times 39) = 51 \times 39$.<br><br>A) $51 \times 39$    B) $50 \times 39$    C) $51 \times 30$    D) $51 \times 30 \times 9$ | 16.<br><br>A |
| 17. A rectangle has 4 sides and a triangle has 3 sides.<br><br>A) pentagon    B) circle        C) square        D) triangle | 17.<br><br>D |
| 18. $1989 = 9 \times 221 = 3 \times 3 \times 221$, so choice C is correct.<br><br>A) 3        B) 9        C) 11        D) 221 | 18.<br><br>C |
| 19. $5 + 10 + 15 + 20 + 25 = 75 = 5 \times (1 + 2 + 3 + 4 + 5)$.<br><br>A) 5        B) 10        C) 15        D) 25 | 19.<br><br>A |
| 20. Since single copies cost 95¢, 8 copies cost $8 \times 95¢ = \$7.60$. Since an 8-issue subscription also costs \$7.60, there is no savings.<br><br>A) \$0.00        B) 95¢        C) \$1.90        D) \$3.80 | 20.<br><br>A |
| 21. The only even whole number which is prime is 2, so there is 1.<br><br>A) 0        B) 1        C) 2        D) 3 | 21.<br><br>B |
| 22. One hour ago the time was 12:15 P.M.; two hours ago the time was 11:15 A.M.; three hours ago the time was 10:15 A.M. Three and one-half hours ago the time was 9:45 A.M.<br><br>A) 8:45 A.M.    B) 9:45 A.M.    C) 10:45 A.M.    D) 4:45 P.M. | 22.<br><br>B |

*Go on to the next page* ▐▐▐▶  **4**

| | | |
|---|---|---|
| 23. | Since a plate of green eggs costs twice as much as a plate of ham, a plate of the eggs costs 10¢. The cost of 2 plates of eggs and 3 plates of ham is $2 \times 10¢ + 3 \times 5¢ = 20¢ + 15¢ = 35¢$.<br><br>A) 40¢     B) 35¢     C) 30¢     D) 25¢ | 23.<br><br>B |
| 24. | If I use 7 Special Shipping Boxes, I can only mail $7 \times 3 = 21$ school yearbooks. I will need 1 more Special Shipping Box for a total of 8 Special Shipping Boxes.<br><br>A) 6     B) 7     C) 8     D) 11 | 24.<br><br>C |
| 25. | The two whole numbers I'm thinking of are 100 and 99. The sum of these numbers is $100 + 99 = 199$. The correct answer is choice C.<br><br>A) 100     B) 101     C) 199     D) 201 | 25.<br><br>C |
| 26. | The given sum is equal to $98 = 7 \times 14$; this is divisible by 14.<br><br>A) 11     B) 12     C) 13     D) 14 | 26.<br><br>D |
| 27. | To find the number of eels Sidney the Seahorse needs to power his house, divide 117 by 3. Since $117 \div 3 = 39$, Sidney needs 39 eels.<br><br>A) 39     B) 117     C) 120     D) 351 | 27.<br><br>A |
| 28. | The 3 large branches split into $3 \times 4 = 12$ small branches. These 12 small branches split into $12 \times 5 = 60$ twigs. The correct answer is choice D.<br><br>A) 5     B) 12     C) 20     D) 60 | 28.<br><br>D |
| 29. | 365 days = 52 weeks 1 day; each date in 1990 is 1 day later.<br><br>A) Saturday     B) Sunday     C) Monday     D) Tuesday | 29.<br><br>C |
| 30. | $(101+100+ \ldots +3+2) - (100+99+ \ldots +2+1) = (101-1) = 100$.<br><br>A) 99     B) 100     C) 101     D) 102 | 30.<br><br>B |

*The end of the contest* ✍️     **4**

# 1989-90 Annual 4th Grade Contest

*Spring, 1990*

**4**

## Contest Information

- **Solutions** Turn the page for detailed contest solutions (written in the question boxes) and letter answers (in the answer columns on the right).

- **Scores** When reviewing these questions, remember *this is a contest, not a test*. There is no "passing" or "failing" score. Few students score as high as 24 points (80% correct); students with even half that, 12 points, *deserve commendation!*

- **Answers & Rating Scale** Turn to page 91 for the letter answers to each question and the rating scale for this contest.

| | | Answers |
|---|---|---|
| 1. | $1 + 9 + 9 + 0 = 10 + 9 = 19.$ <br> A) 10     B) 19     C) 109     D) 1990 | 1. <br> B |
| 2. | Together, the vowels and the consonants form all the letters in our alphabet. Our alphabet has 26 letters. <br> A) 26     B) 30     C) 31     D) 32 | 2. <br> A |
| 3. | $(19 \times 100) + (9 \times 10) = 1900 + 90 = 1990.$ <br> A) 280     B) 1909     C) 1990     D) 2880 | 3. <br> C |
| 4. | $49 + 23 = 72.$ <br> A) 72     B) 62     C) 26     D) 16 | 4. <br> A |
| 5. | Only a 10 will make the numbers the same on both sides. <br> A) 15     B) 14     C) 12     D) 10 | 5. <br> D |
| 6. | Since Ronnie has 12 *pairs* of shoes, Ronnie has $12 \times 2 = 24$ shoes. <br> A) 6     B) 12     C) 14     D) 24 | 6. <br> D |
| 7. | $1 + 11 + 111 + 1111 = 1234.$ <br> A) 11111     B) 1111     C) 4321     D) 1234 | 7. <br> D |
| 8. | $(2 \times 24) \div 4 = 48 \div 4 = 12.$ <br> A) 3     B) 6     C) 12     D) 18 | 8. <br> C |
| 9. | The *average* is 888, so $777 + 888 + 999 = 3 \times 888 = 2664.$ <br> A) 2664     B) 2554     C) 2464     D) 2444 | 9. <br> A |
| 10. | Since each of the two parents' meals cost $10, the parents spent $20 for their meals. Since each of the three children ordered the $3 special children's meal, the children's meals cost a total of $9. The total spent was $20 + $9 = $29. <br> A) $13     B) $23     C) $29     D) $36 | 10. <br> C |
| 11. | Since $5 - 5 = 0$, the answer is B. <br> A) $5 + 5$     B) $5 - 5$     C) $5 \times 5$     D) $5 \div 5$ | 11. <br> B |

*Go on to the next page* ⏭ **4**

| | | | |
|---|---|---|---|
| 12. | $(1 \div 1) \times (2 \div 2) \times (3 \div 3) \times (4 \div 4) = 1 \times 1 \times 1 \times 1 = 1.$ | | 12. |
| | A) 1    B) 4    C) 10    D) 24 | | A |

| | |
|---|---|
| 13. | Joel's phone rings for $5 \times 3 = 15$ seconds. We *don't* count the silence *after* the final ring, so there are only 4 periods of silence. This takes $4 \times 2 = 8$ seconds. From the start of the 1st until the end of the 5th ring takes $15 + 8 = 23$ seconds. |
| | A) 15 seconds   B) 17 seconds   C) 23 seconds   D) 25 seconds |

13.

C

| | |
|---|---|
| 14. | $(2 + 4 + 6 + 8) \div (1 + 2 + 3 + 4) = 20 \div 10 = 2.$ |
| | A) 1    B) 4    C) 10    D) 2 |

14.

D

| | |
|---|---|
| 15. | A triangle has 3 sides and a square has 4 sides. The product of 3 and 4 is 12. |
| | A) 7    B) 8    C) 12    D) 16 |

15.

C

| | |
|---|---|
| 16. | $(24 + 48 + 96) \div 3 = 168 \div 3 = 56.$ |
| | A) 48    B) 52    C) 55    D) 56 |

16.

D

| | |
|---|---|
| 17. | The first ten odd whole numbers are 1, 3, 5, 7, 9, 11, 13, 15, 17, and 19. The tenth odd whole number is 19. |
| | A) 21    B) 19    C) 17    D) 11 |

17.

B

| | |
|---|---|
| 18. | Lee has $1 \times 25¢ + 2 \times 10¢ + 1 \times 1¢ = 25¢ + 20¢ + 1¢ = 46¢.$ |
| | A) 36¢    B) 37¢    C) 46¢    D) 61¢ |

18.

C

| | |
|---|---|
| 19. | Since 1 m = 100 cm, a 3 m piece of string is 300 cm long. Divide 300 by 30 to get 10, the number of pieces. |
| | A) 3    B) 10    C) 90    D) 100 |

19.
B

| | |
|---|---|
| 20. | The greatest whole number that divides 36 and 90 is 18. |
| | A) 3    B) 9    C) 18    D) 90 |

20.

C

| | |
|---|---|
| 21. | Since the line extends forever in both directions, it crosses (intersects) the circle 2 times. |
| | A) 0    B) 1    C) 2    D) 3 |

21.

C

*Go on to the next page* ⅢⅢ➡ **4**

| | | | | |
|---|---|---|---|---|
| 22. | From page 20 to page 29 is 10 pages. From page 30 to page 39 is another 10 pages. Page 40 is 1 more page. All together, Dale read 10 + 10 + 1 = 21 pages.<br><br>A) 40     B) 21     C) 20     D) 19 | | | 22.<br><br>B |
| 23. | In 1 hour, it'll be 12:15 P.M.; 7 minutes earlier is 12:08 P.M.<br><br>A) 12:08 P.M.   B) 12:13 P.M.   C) 1:03 P.M.   D) 12:08 A.M. | | | 23.<br><br>A |
| 24. | Multiply the *ones'* digits: 1×2×3×4×5 = 120, so D is correct.<br><br>A) 3×6×7×8×9×11     B) 11×21×31×41×51<br><br>C) 15×25×35×45     D) 11×22×33×44×55 | | | 24.<br><br>D |
| 25. | Gerry could have one penny and four nickels. Then, the amount of money Gerry would have is 1¢ + 20¢ = 21¢.<br><br>A) 5¢     B) 16¢     C) 21¢     D) 42¢ | | | 25.<br><br>C |
| 26. | John will be 10 years old in 3 years, so he is now 7. Mary is 2 years younger than John, so she is now 5 years old.<br><br>A) 8     B) 7     C) 6     D) 5 | | | 26.<br><br>D |
| 27. | If I buy 6 packages, I only get 6×4 = 24 apples. But if I buy 7 packages, I get 7×4 = 28 apples. So the answer is B.<br><br>A) 6     B) 7     C) 8     D) 12 | | | 27.<br><br>B |
| 28. | Two days after Monday is Wednesday.<br><br>A) Wednesday   B) Thursday    C) Friday     D) Saturday | | | 28.<br><br>A |
| 29. | Lee paints the room once in 6 hours. Pat paints the room twice in 6 hours. Together, they paint the room 3 times in 6 hours. So, it takes them 2 hours to paint it once together.<br><br>A) 2 hours    B) 3 hours    C) 9 hours    D) 18 hours | | | 29.<br><br>A |
| 30. | There are six such numbers: 123, 132, 213, 231, 312, and 321. (Numbers like 223 don't use all three digits.)<br><br>A) 3     B) 6     C) 123     D) 300 | | | 30.<br><br>B |

*The end of the contest* 🖎   **4**

## Solutions

# 1990-91 Annual 4th Grade Contest
*Spring, 1991*

**4**

## Contest Information

- **Solutions** Turn the page for detailed contest solutions (written in the question boxes) and letter answers (in the answer columns on the right).

- **Scores** When reviewing these questions, remember *this is a contest, not a test*. There is no "passing" or "failing" score. Few students score as high as 24 points (80% correct); students with even half that, 12 points, *deserve commendation!*

- **Answers & Rating Scale** Turn to page 92 for the letter answers to each question and the rating scale for this contest.

## *1990-91 4TH GRADE CONTEST SOLUTIONS*

| | *Answers* |
|---|---|
| 1. $19 + 91 = 10 + 9 + 91 = 10 + (9 + 91) = 10 + 100 = 110$.<br>A) 100 B) 101 C) 110 D) 1991 | 1.<br>C |
| 2. Since $7 \times 3¢ = 21¢$, you can buy 7 stamps.<br>A) 7 B) 18 C) 24 D) 63 | 2.<br>A |
| 3. $1 \times (1 + 1) \times (1 + 1 + 1) = 1 \times 2 \times 3 = 6$.<br>A) 1 B) 3 C) 5 D) 6 | 3.<br>D |
| 4. 9898 is only 2 less than 9900.<br>A) 9800 B) 9890 C) 9900 D) 9990 | 4.<br>C |
| 5. In adding 1234 + 4321, every column has a sum of 5.<br>A) 4444 B) 4567 C) 4765 D) 5555 | 5.<br>D |
| 6. $8 \times 8 = 64$, so the missing number is 1.<br>A) 1 B) 2 C) 4 D) 64 | 6.<br>A |
| 7. In square *ABCD* shown at the right, $AB = 3$, so every side is 3, and the perimeter is $4 \times 3 = 12$.  <br>A) 3 B) 6 C) 9 D) 12 | 7.<br>D |
| 8. 25 nickels = 5 quarters, since $25 \times 5 = 5 \times 25$.<br>A) 1 B) 5 C) 25 D) 125 | 8.<br>B |
| 9. $12 \div (5 - 2) = 12 \div 3 = 4$.<br>A) 1 B) 3 C) 4 D) 9 | 9.<br>C |
| 10. An even number must end in 0, 2, 4, 6, or 8.<br>A) 1234 B) 4321 C) 2413 D) 4231 | 10.<br>A |
| 11. $(1 \times 100)+(10 \times 10)+(100 \times 1) = 100+100+100 = 300$.<br>A) 100 B) 111 C) 220 D) 300 | 11.<br>D |
| 12. 6 has 1, 2, 3, and 6 as factors; 4 has only 1, 2, and 4.<br>A) 1 B) 3 C) 4 D) 6 | 12.<br>C |

*Go on to the next page* ➡ **4**

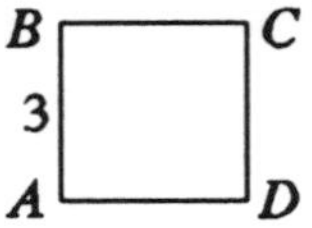

| | | Answers |
|---|---|---|
| 13. | $25 + 25 + 25 + 25 + 25 = 5 \times 25 = 25 \times 5.$ <br> A) $25 \times 25$    B) $25 + 5$    C) $25 \div 5$    D) $25 \times 5$ | 13. <br> D |
| 14. | If I travel 1 km north, then 1 km east, then 1 km south, I must go 1 km west to reach my starting point. <br> A) 0 km    B) 1 km    C) 2 km    D) 3 km | 14. <br> B |
| 15. | $(3 + 3) \times (3 - 3) \times (3 \div 3) = 6 \times 0 \times 1 = 0.$ <br> A) 0    B) 3    C) 6    D) 9 | 15. <br> A |
| 16. | If four times a number is 20, then two times that same number is half as much, which is 10. <br> A) 5    B) 10    C) 20    D) 40 | 16. <br> B |
| 17. | $2 \times 2 \times 2 \times 5 \times 5 \times 5 = 2 \times 5 \times 2 \times 5 \times 2 \times 5 = 10 \times 10 \times 10 = 1000.$ <br> A) 100    B) 200    C) 500    D) 1000 | 17. <br> D |
| 18. | Since $9+9+9 = 27$, the ones' digit is a 7. <br> A) 2    B) 7    C) 8    D) 9 | 18. <br> B |
| 19. | In $123+231+312$, the sum in every column is a 6. <br> A) 456    B) 555    C) 567    D) 666 | 19. <br> D |
| 20. | If the product of two whole numbers is 5, then one of the numbers is 5 and the other is 1. Their sum is 6. <br> A) 10    B) 6    C) 5    D) 4 | 20. <br> B |
| 21. | If the store were open from 7 A.M. till 7 P.M., it would be open 12 hours each day; so 1 hour more is 13 hours. <br> A) 8    B) 12    C) 13    D) 15 | 21. <br> C |
| 22. | $111 \times 111 = 12321.$ <br> A) 11111    B) 12321    C) 12345    D) 14641 | 22. <br> B |
| 23. | The sum of the ages of Tom, Dick, and Harry is 26. If Tom is 9 and Dick is 10, then Harry is $26 - 9 - 10 = 17 - 10 = 7.$ <br> A) 7    B) 11    C) 16    D) 17 | 23. <br> A |

*Go on to the next page* ⫸ **4**

| | |
|---|---|
| 24. The largest whole number which, when multiplied by 3, is less than 25 is 8, since $3 \times 8 = 24$.<br><br>A) 7      B) 8      C) 9      D) 24 | 24.<br>B |
| 25. There are two whole numbers each less than 100 whose sum is 197. These numbers are 98 and 99. The difference between the two numbers is $99 - 98 = 1$.<br><br>A) 0      B) 1      C) 2      D) 3 | 25.<br>B |
| 26. If the film begins at 1:45 P.M., then 1 hour 15 minutes later would be 3 P.M. The film lasts another 3 minutes, so it ends at 3:03 P.M.<br><br>A) 2:03 P.M.   B) 2:18 P.M.   C) 3:03 P.M.   D) 3:18 P.M. | 26.<br>C |
| 27. Regrouping, $(98+102) + (99+101) + 100 = 500$.<br><br>A) 497      B) 498      C) 499      D) 500 | 27.<br>D |
| 28. If doubling the number of pennies gives me 12¢ more, then I must have 12 pennies.<br><br>A) 12      B) 7      C) 5      D) 2 | 28.<br>A |
| 29. In 12 hrs, an hour hand goes around once. A minute hand goes around once each hour, so in 12 hrs, it goes around 12 times.<br><br>A) 12 times   B) 24 times   C) 60 times   D) 720 times | 29.<br>A |
| 30. The number of different triangles in the diagram is 5. There are 4 small triangles, and there is also the large triangle itself. 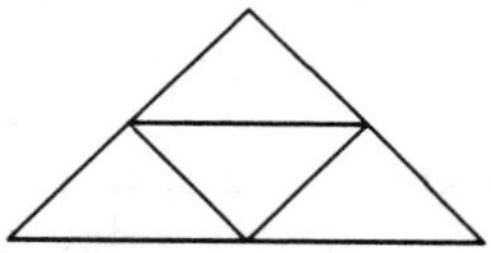<br><br>A) 1      B) 4      C) 5      D) 6 | 30.<br>C |

*The end of the contest* ✍  **4**

56

# Solutions

## 1988-89 Annual 5th Grade Contest
*Spring, 1989*

**5**

### Contest Information

- **Solutions** Turn the page for detailed contest solutions (written in the question boxes) and letter answers (in the answer columns on the right).

- **Scores** When reviewing these questions, remember *this is a contest, not a test*. There is no "passing" or "failing" score. Few students score as high as 24 points (80% correct); students with even half that, 12 points, *deserve commendation!*

- **Answers & Rating Scale** Turn to page 93 for the letter answers to each question and the rating scale for this contest.

| | | | | | Answers |
|---|---|---|---|---|---|
| 1. | Since $1989 \div 9 = 221$, $1989 = 9 \times 221$. | | | | 1. |
| | A) 111 | B) 121 | C) 211 | D) 221 | D |
| 2. | $0 + 100 = 100$, so choice A is correct. | | | | 2. |
| | A) $0 + 100$ | B) $0 \times 100$ | C) $0 \div 100$ | D) $100 - 100$ | A |
| 3. | $1 \times 1 \times 1 \times 1 \times 9 \times 1 \times 1 \times 1 \times 1 = 1 \times 9 \times 1 = 9$. | | | | 3. |
| | A) 9 | B) 17 | C) 72 | D) 81 | A |
| 4. | $2000 - 1989 = 11$; no other choice is closer than this. | | | | 4. |
| | A) 989 | B) 1889 | C) 1970 | D) 2000 | D |
| 5. | Regroup: $98 + 2 + 98 + 2 + 98 + 2 + 98 + 2 + 98 + 2 = 500$. | | | | 5. |
| | A) 495 | B) 500 | C) 505 | D) 999 | B |
| 6. | 10 pennies = 10¢ and 10 nickels = 50¢. The value is 60¢. | | | | 6. |
| | A) 20¢ | B) 50¢ | C) 60¢ | D) $1.10 | C |
| 7. | $4321 + 5678 = 9999$, so the correct answer is choice D. | | | | 7. |
| | A) 9889 | B) 9009 | C) 10009 | D) 9999 | D |
| 8. | No matter how many pieces the string is cut into, the sum of of the lengths of all of the pieces is *always* 12. | | | | 8. D |
| | A) 3 | B) 4 | C) 9 | D) 12 | |
| 9. | The 1st sum is 9 more than the 2nd sum, so the difference is 9. | | | | 9. |
| | A) 0 | B) 1 | C) 9 | D) 79 | C |
| 10. | The numbers from 1 to 100 that are divisible by 3 are $1 \times 3$, $2 \times 3$, $3 \times 3$, . . . , $32 \times 3$, and $33 \times 3$. There are 33 such numbers. | | | | 10. C |
| | A) 3 | B) 30 | C) 33 | D) 34 | |
| 11. | The square of 4 is $4 \times 4 = 16$. | | | | 11. |
| | A) 2 | B) 8 | C) 16 | D) 44 | C |

*Go on to the next page* ▮▮▮➡ **5**

| | |
|---|---|
| 12. The difference between my parents' ages is always the same. So, four years ago the difference was 10 years.<br><br>A) 2 years    B) 6 years    C) 10 years    D) 14 years | 12.<br>C |
| 13. The sum of ten 99's is the same as 10 × 99.<br><br>A) 10 × 99    B) 10 + 99    C) 9 × 99    D) 99 × 99 | 13.<br><br>A |
| 14. The Speedo Car Co. charges $8400 for a car, but gives a $600 rebate. The real cost of the car, *after* the rebate but *before* taxes is $8400 − $600 = $7800.<br><br>A) $2400    B) $7800    C) $8400    D) $9000 | 14.<br><br><br>B |
| 15. 12 × 34 + 56 ÷ 7 = (12 × 34) + (56 ÷ 7) = 408 + 8 = 416.<br><br>A) 464 ÷ 7    B) 1080 ÷ 7    C) 504    D) 416 | 15.<br><br>D |
| 16. 34 + 1 is not prime, even, or divisible by 3; new number is odd.<br><br>A) prime                        B) divisible by 3<br>C) even                        D) odd | 16.<br><br>D |
| 17. The first 3 minutes of this call costs 20¢; the next 7 minutes costs 7×5¢ = 35¢. The total cost is 20¢ + 35¢ = 55¢.<br><br>A) 25¢    B) 55¢    C) 65¢    D) 95¢ | 17.<br>B |
| 18. The average is (1 + 2 + 3 + 4 + 5 + 6 + 7)÷7 = 28÷7 = 4.<br><br>A) 1    B) 4    C) 7    D) 28 | 18.<br><br>B |
| 19. Rearrange as 1000×0.001×100×0.01×10×0.1×1 = 1×1×1×1 = 1.<br><br>A) 0    B) 0.1    C) 1    D) 10 | 19.<br><br>C |
| 20. A rectangle has 4 sides and so does a rhombus.<br><br>A) a triangle    B) a rhombus    C) a circle    D) a pentagon | 20.<br>B |
| 21. 12 : 3 = 4 : 1 = (5×4) : (5×1) = 20 : 5.<br>A) 4    B) 5    C) 6    D) 8 | 21.<br><br>B |

*Go on to the next page* ⟫⟫ **5**

| | | | |
|---|---|---|---|
| 22. | Any integer ending in 5 is divisible by 5; the only prime is 5. | | 22. |
| | A) 0　　　　B) 1　　　　C) 5　　　　D) 25 | | B |
| 23. | 1 hour = 60 minutes = 60×60 seconds = 3600 seconds. Since 32 "frames" are shown each second, the number of "frames" in a one-hour movie is 32×3600. | | 23. D |
| | A) 3600　　B) 32 × 60　　C) 32 × 360　　D) 32 × 3600 | | |
| 24. | $\frac{22}{33} = \frac{2 \times 11}{3 \times 11} = \frac{2}{3} = \frac{2 \times 10}{3 \times 10} = \frac{20}{30} = \frac{2}{3} = \frac{2 \times 2}{3 \times 2} = \frac{4}{6}.$ | | 24. |
| | A) $\frac{22}{33}$　　B) $\frac{20}{30}$　　C) $\frac{4}{6}$　　D) $\frac{12}{13}$ | | D |
| 25. | The two-digit number is greater than or equal to 50 and less than 60. All such numbers round up to 100. | | 25. C |
| | A) 0　　　　B) 50　　　　C) 100　　　　D) 150 | | |
| 26. | Both the square and the equilateral triangle have all sides equal. The perimeter of the shaded figure *ABECD* is 5×4 = 20. | | 26. B |
| | A) 16　　　　B) 20　　　　C) 24　　　　D) 28 | | |
| 27. | The only years from 1990 to 2800 with a *digital sum* of 27 are 1998 and 2799, so the correct answer is choice C. | | 27. C |
| | A) 0　　　　B) 1　　　　C) 2　　　　D) 3 | | |
| 28. | If I start with $100 and increase this by 50%, I have $150. If I then decrease this by 50%, I will have $75. | | 28. C |
| | A) $50　　　B) $66　　　C) $75　　　D) $100 | | |
| 29. | 3600 seconds = 60 minutes = 1 hour; the time is 12:30 P.M. | | 29. |
| | A) 12:30 P.M.　B) 2:30 P.M.　C) 7:30 P.M.　D) 1:30 A.M. | | A |
| 30. | 366 days = 52 weeks 2 days; this date in 1988 is 2 days earlier. | | 30. |
| | A) a Friday　B) a Saturday　C) a Sunday　D) a Monday | | A |

*The end of the contest* ✍🏻  **5**

## Solutions

# 1989-90 Annual 5th Grade Contest
*Spring, 1990*

**5**

## Contest Information

- **Solutions** Turn the page for detailed contest solutions (written in the question boxes) and letter answers (in the answer columns on the right).

- **Scores** When reviewing these questions, remember *this is a contest, not a test*. There is no "passing" or "failing" score. Few students score as high as 24 points (80% correct); students with even half that, 12 points, *deserve commendation!*

- **Answers & Rating Scale** Turn to page 94 for the letter answers to each question and the rating scale for this contest.

| | | |
|---|---|---|
| 1. | $1000 + 900 + 90 + 0 = 1900 + 90 = 1990$.<br><br>A) 2000     B) 1990     C) 199     D) 0 | 1.<br>B |
| 2. | The value of 1 penny, 5 nickels, and 10 dimes is $1\times1\text{¢}$<br>$+ 5\times5\text{¢} + 10\times10\text{¢} = 1\text{¢} + 25\text{¢} + 100\text{¢} = 126\text{¢} = \$1.26$.<br><br>A) \$1.25     B) \$1.26     C) \$1.51     D) \$1.60 | 2.<br>B |
| 3. | $5 + (5 \times 5) - (5 \div 5) = 5 + 25 - 1 = 29$.<br><br>A) 29     B) 25     C) 23     D) 9 | 3.<br>A |
| 4. | The numeral for one million is 1 000 000. This<br>numeral has seven digits.<br><br>A) one million   B) ten     C) seven     D) six | 4.<br>C |
| 5. | Since 1992 is 2 more than 1990, the remainder is 2.<br><br>A) 1     B) 2     C) 1990     D) 1992 | 5.<br>B |
| 6. | $3000 = 30 \times 100$, so the answer is C.<br><br>A) 10     B) 30     C) 100     D) 300 | 6.<br>C |
| 7. | $9\times8 + 8\times9 = 72 + 72 = 144$.<br><br>A) 72     B) 144     C) 187     D) 9889 | 7.<br>B |
| 8. | $(45+55)+(45+55)+(45+55)+(45+55)+(45+55) = 5\times100 = 500$.<br><br>A) 400     B) 450     C) 500     D) 555 | 8.<br>C |
| 9. | Since $51 = 3 \times 17$, choice C is correct.<br><br>A) 49     B) 50     C) 51     D) 52 | 9.<br>C |
| 10. | $1919 \div 19 = 101$, so the answer is D.<br><br>A) 10     B) 11     C) 100     D) 101 | 10.<br>D |
| 11. | $1 \times 9 \times 9 \times 0 = 0$.<br><br>A) 0     B) 1     C) 19     D) 81 | 11.<br>A |
| 12. | $2 + 3 + 5 + 7 = 17$. (Note: 1 is *not* a prime number.)<br><br>A) 10     B) 11     C) 16     D) 17 | 12.<br>D |

*Go on to the next page* ⮕ **5**

| | | | | |
|---|---|---|---|---|
| 13. | $2 + 22 + 222 + 2222 = 2468$, so the answer is choice A. | | | 13. |
| | A) 2468    B) 4444    C) 8642    D) 8888 | | | A |
| 14. | Jill arrived 20 minutes before 2:13 P.M. 13 minutes before 2:13 P.M. is 2 P.M.; and 7 minutes before that is 1:53 P.M. | | | 14. |
| | A) 1:43 P.M.    B) 1:47 P.M.    C) 1:53 P.M.    D) 1:57 P.M. | | | C |
| 15. | $15 + 15 + 15 + 15 + 15 = 75 = 5 \times 15$. | | | 15. |
| | A) 75    B) 15    C) 12    D) 3 | | | B |
| 16. | Since the product of 2 *consecutive* whole numbers is 56, the numbers must be 7 and 8. Their *sum* is $7 + 8 = 15$. | | | 16. |
| | A) 7    B) 11    C) 14    D) 15 | | | D |
| 17. | Only a 2 will make the numbers the same on both sides. | | | 17. |
| | A) 2    B) 3    C) 4    D) 6 | | | A |
| 18. | The only number which will be equal to itself after being doubled is 0. Thus, Paul's original number was a 0. | | | 18. |
| | A) 0    B) 1    C) 2    D) 4 | | | A |
| 19. | $(6 + 60 + 600) \div 3 = 666 \div 3 = 222$. | | | 19. |
| | A) 666    B) 333    C) 222    D) 111 | | | C |
| 20. | Since $6 \times 6 = 36$, the whole number that Alexandra multiplied by itself was 6. | | | 20. |
| | A) 4    B) 6    C) 9    D) 36 | | | B |
| 21. | Since 11 is prime, its only factors are itself and 1. The other numbers, 6, 8, and 10, all have more than two factors. | | | 21. |
| | A) 6    B) 8    C) 10    D) 11 | | | D |
| 22. | The multiples of 100 which are closest to 1990 are 1900 and 2000. Since 1990 is closer to 2000 than 1900, the answer is D. | | | 22. |
| | A) 1900    B) 1990    C) 1995    D) 2000 | | | D |

*Go on to the next page* ▐▐▐➡ **5**

| | | |
|---|---|---|
| 23. | Since $2 \times 2 \times 2 \times 2 \times 2 \times 2 = 64$, the answer is B. | 23.<br><br>B |
| | A) 5  B) 6  C) 7  D) 32 | |
| 24. | Since *YOURS + MINE* is equal to *YOURS − MINE*, the value of *MINE* is 0. | 24.<br><br>A |
| | A) 0  B) 1  C) 2  D) 10 | |
| 25. | Since the average of three *consecutive* whole numbers is 24, these numbers must be 23, 24, and 25. | 25.<br><br>C |
| | A) 22  B) 24  C) 25  D) 26 | |
| 26. | Six years ago, my parents were *each* 6 years younger, so the sum of their ages was 70 − 6 − 6 = 58. | 26.<br><br>A |
| | A) 58  B) 64  C) 70  D) 76 | |
| 27. | Since Ali was tenth, 9 students got grades higher than hers *and* 9 students got grades lower than hers. Including Ali, there are $9 + 9 + 1 = 19$ students in the class. | 27.<br><br>B |
| | A) 10  B) 19  C) 20  D) 21 | |
| 28. | $9 \times 9 \times 9 \times 9 \times 9 \times 9 \times 9 \times 9 = 81 \times 81 \times 81 \times 81$. The ones' digit is 1. | 28.<br><br>A |
| | A) 1  B) 2  C) 8  D) 9 | |
| 29. | All the numbers that Joan counted left remainders of 2 when divided by 7. Of the numbers listed, only 15 does *not* leave a remainder of 2 when divided by 7. | 29.<br><br>D |
| | A) 65  B) 30  C) 23  D) 15 | |
| 30. | For *each* 1st letter, there are 6 arrangements. For example, with *S* first, we get: *STOP, STPO, SOTP, SOPT, SPTO, SPOT.* Therefore, the total number of different ways is $4 \times 6 = 24$. | 30.<br><br>D |
| | A) 4  B) 6  C) 12  D) 24 | |

*The end of the contest*  ✍  **5**

# Solutions

## 1990-91 Annual 5th Grade Contest

*Spring, 1991*

**5**

### Contest Information

■ **Solutions** Turn the page for detailed contest solutions (written in the question boxes) and letter answers (in the answer columns on the right).

■ **Scores** When reviewing these questions, remember *this is a contest, not a test*. There is no "passing" or "failing" score. Few students score as high as 24 points (80% correct); students with even half that, 12 points, *deserve commendation!*

■ **Answers & Rating Scale** Turn to page 95 for the letter answers to each question and the rating scale for this contest.

1. $1 \times 9 \times 9 \times 1 = (1 \times 9) \times (9 \times 1) = 9 \times 9 = 81$.

   A) $1 \times 9$      B) $9 \times 9$      C) $1 \times 1$      D) $19 \times 19$

   1.

   B

2. In the diagram shown at the right, line segment *AB* is a diameter of the circle. The length of a radius is half that of a diameter, so the radius is 5.

   A) 5      B) 10      C) 20      D) $10\pi$

   2.

   A

3. $2 - 2 + 2 - 2 + 2 = (2 - 2) + (2 - 2) + 2 = 0 + 0 + 2 = 2$.

   A) 10      B) 4      C) 2      D) 0

   3.

   C

4. The even digits are 0, 2, 4, 6, and 8. The product of all of these even digits is 0.

   A) 384      B) 48      C) 32      D) 0

   4.

   D

5. $11 \times 11 \times 11 = (11 \times 11) \times 11 = 121 \times 11 = 1331$.

   A) 1111      B) 1221      C) 1331      D) 1441

   5.

   C

6. $(4 - 1) \times (4 - 2) \times (4 - 3) \times (4 - 4) = 3 \times 2 \times 1 \times 0 = 0$.

   A) 0      B) 6      C) 24      D) 256

   6.

   A

7. Since $8 \times 8 = 64$ and $16 \times 4 = 64$, the missing number is 4.

   A) 16      B) 4      C) 2      D) 1

   7.

   B

8. A pizza costs \$6 and a soda costs 75¢. The total cost of 2 pizzas and 4 sodas is $(2 \times \$6) + (4 \times 75¢) = \$12 + \$3 = \$15$.

   A) \$13.50      B) \$15.00      C) \$25.50      D) \$27.00

   8.

   B

9. $9880 \div 8 = 1235$.

   A) 1234      B) 1235      C) 1236      D) 1237

   9.

   B

10. The product increases as both numbers get more nearly equal.

    A) $7 \times 13$      B) $8 \times 12$      C) $9 \times 11$      D) $10 \times 10$

    10.

    D

11. $(1 \times 1) + (10 \times 10) + (100 \times 100) = 1 + 100 + 10000 = 10101$.

    A) 111      B) 1001      C) 10101      D) 10201

    11.

    C

*Go on to the next page* ⫸    **5**

| | | |
|---|---|---|
| 12. | The perimeter of the rectangle in the diagram is 20 and the width is 4. Since 20–4–4 = 12, 12 is left for the two lengths, so each length is 6.    4 ▭ <br><br>A) 5      B) 6      C) 16      D) 24 | 12. <br><br> B |
| 13. | 4321 – 1234 = 3087. <br><br>A) 2222      B) 2345      C) 3087      D) 3187 | 13. <br><br> C |
| 14. | The ones' digit of 987 × 789 equals the ones' digit of 7 × 9, a 3. <br><br>A) 1      B) 3      C) 7      D) 9 | 14. <br><br> B |
| 15. | (111+111+111+111) – (11+11+11+11) = 444 – 44 = 400. <br><br>A) 44      B) 400      C) 444      D) 1111 | 15. <br><br> B |
| 16. | The number of sides of a square multiplied by the number of vertices of a square is 4 × 4 = 16. <br><br>A) 8      B) 9      C) 12      D) 16 | 16. <br><br> D |
| 17. | (19 × 91)–(19 × 90) = 91 nineteens – 90 nineteens = one 19. <br><br>A) 19      B) 90      C) 1990      D) 1 | 17. <br><br> A |
| 18. | In 60 minutes there are 60 × 60 = 3600 seconds. <br><br>A) 1      B) 60      C) 3000      D) 3600 | 18. <br><br> D |
| 19. | 5 × (3+4) = (5 × 3) + (5 × 4) = (5 × 3) + 20. <br><br>A) 4      B) 12      C) 15      D) 20 | 19. <br><br> D |
| 20. | Each angle in a rectangle is a right angle, 90°. <br><br>A) 90°      B) 60°      C) acute      D) obtuse | 20. <br><br> A |
| 21. | If Huey is 12 years old, then Donald is twice as old, 24. Since Mickey is twice as old as Donald, Mickey is 48. <br><br>A) 3      B) 6      C) 24      D) 48 | 21. <br><br> D |
| 22. | When a certain whole number is divided by 5, the remainder is odd. The original whole number must end in a 1, 3, 6, or 8. <br><br>A) 41      B) 47      C) 54      D) 59 | 22. <br><br> A |

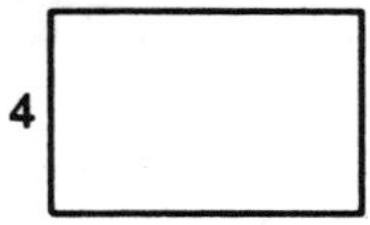

*Go on to the next page* ⫸ **5**

| | | Answers |
|---|---|---|
| 23. | I earn $5 an hour. If I work 5 hours a day for 5 days, then I have worked 25 hours and I earned $25 \times \$5 = \$125$.<br><br>A) $5    B) $25    C) $125    D) $555 | 23.<br><br>C |
| 24. | Since the quotient was 663 and the remainder was 2, the original number was $(3 \times 663) + 2 = 1989 + 2 = 1991$.<br><br>A) 666    B) 669    C) 1990    D) 1991 | 24.<br><br>D |
| 25. | I am 5 years older than my brother. If he is now 21, then I am now 26. In 5 years, I will be 31 years old.<br><br>A) 16    B) 26    C) 31    D) 36 | 25.<br><br>C |
| 26. | Counting both 9 and 999, there are 111 multiples of 9 from 9 through 999. Excluding 9 and 999 leaves only 109 numbers.<br><br>A) 108    B) 109    C) 110    D) 111 | 26.<br><br>B |
| 27. | When we divide by 2, 3, or 5, the remainder is 1. Hence, if we *first* subtract 1, the result will be divisible by 2, 3, and 5.<br><br>A) 31    B) 16    C) 11    D) 7 | 27.<br><br>A |
| 28. | If I have an equal number of pennies and nickels and no other coins, I can split my money into 6¢ portions. The amount of money I have must be divisible by 6.<br><br>A) 24¢    B) 25¢    C) 26¢    D) 27¢ | 28.<br><br>A |
| 29. | If $2+4+6+ \ldots +196+198+200 = 10100$, then the value of $1+2+3+ \ldots +98+99+100$ is half of $10\,100$, namely 5050.<br><br>A) 1000    B) 5000    C) 5050    D) 10000 | 29.<br><br>C |
| 30. | In the diagram, there are four 1 by 1 rectangles, two 2 by 1 rectangles, two 1 by 2 rectangles, and one 2 by 2 rectangle. The number of rectangles is 9.<br><br>A) 4    B) 5    C) 9    D) 10 | 30.<br><br>C |

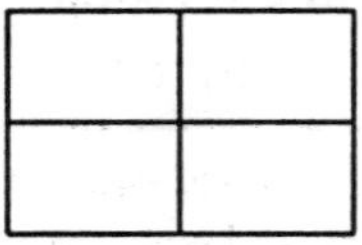

*The end of the contest* 🖉 **5**

# Solutions

## 1986-87 Annual 6th Grade Contest

*Tuesday, March 3, 1987*

**6**

### Contest Information

- **Solutions** Turn the page for detailed contest solutions (written in the question boxes) and letter answers (in the answer columns on the right).

- **Scores** When reviewing these questions, remember *this is a contest, not a test*. There is no "passing" or "failing" score. Few students score as high as 30 points (75% correct); students with even half that, 15 points, *deserve commendation!*

- **Answers & Rating Scale** Turn to page 96 for the letter answers to each question and the rating scale for this contest.

| | |
|---|---|
| 1. $83 + 83 + 83 + 17 + 17 + 17 + 17 = 100 + 100 + 100 + 17 = 317.$ | 1. |
|    A) 300        B) 317        C) 383        D) 400 | B |
| 2. If the average of two numbers is 7, their sum is $2 \times 7 = 14.$ | 2. |
|    A) 3 and 4     B) 1 and 8     C) 2 and 14     D) 6 and 8 | D |
| 3. An even number multiplied by an odd number is even. | 3. |
|    A) $666 + 777$   B) $666 - 555$   C) $666 \times 333$   D) $666 \div 222$ | C |
| 4. $(0 \times 1) + (0 \times 2) + (0 \times 3) + (0 \times 4) = 0 + 0 + 0 + 0 = 0.$ | 4. |
|    A) 0         B) 10        C) 24        D) 25 | A |
| 5. The degree-measure of each angle of a square is $90°$. | 5. |
|    A) $4°$        B) $90°$        C) $100°$        D) $360°$ | B |
| 6. $88888 - 9999 = 88888 - 10000 + 1 = 78888 + 1 = 78889.$ | 6. |
|    A) 11111       B) 78889       C) 77889       D) 79999 | B |
| 7. Since their product is 66, the numbers could be 1 and 66. The correct answer is D. | 7. |
|    A) 11        B) 22        C) 33        D) 66 | D |
| 8. $14 \times 15 \times 16 = 14 \times 15 \times 2 \times 2 \times 4 = 14 \times 2 \times 15 \times 2 \times 4 = 28 \times 30 \times 4.$ | 8. |
|    A) 2        B) 4        C) 8        D) 32 | B |
| 9. Since the hundreds' digit is 4, round 5499 down to 5000. | 9. |
|    A) 5000       B) 5400       C) 5500       D) 6000 | A |
| 10. $1^1 + 1^2 + 1^3 + 1^4 = 1 + 1 + 1 + 1 = 4.$ | 10. |
|    A) 4        B) 10        C) 14        D) 50 | A |
| 11. $(3 \times 5 \times 7) - (3 \times 5) = (3 \times 5 \times 7) - (3 \times 5 \times 1) = 3 \times 5 \times 6.$ | 11. |
|    A) 7       B) $3 \times 5 \times 1$   C) $3 \times 5 \times 6$   D) $3 \times 5 \times 7$ | C |
| 12. $10¢ : 25¢ = 10 : 25 = (10 \times 4) : (25 \times 4) = 40 : 100 = 40\%.$ | 12. |
|    A) 2/5%      B) 10%      C) 40%      D) 250% | C |
| 13. $(5 \times 10) + (7 \times 1) + (4 \times 1000) + (3 \times 100) = 50 + 7 + 4000 + 300 = 4357.$ | 13. |
|    A) 5743       B) 3457       C) 4357       D) 4537 | C |
| 14. Jill is now 14. Two years ago, she was 12. Since Jack is now 6 years older than Jill was 2 years ago, Jack is now $12 + 6 = 18.$ | 14. |
|    A) 10        B) 18        C) 20        D) 22 | B |
| 15. The average is $(99 + 97 + 95 + 93 + 91) \div 5 = (95 \times 5) \div 5 = 95.$ | 15. |
|    A) 95        B) 94        C) 95.5        D) 94.5 | A |

*Go on to the next page* ‖▶ **6**

| | | |
|---|---|---|
| 16. | Since the perimeter of the triangle is 24, each side is $24 \div 3 = 8$. But this is also the length of a side of the square. So, its perimeter is $4 \times 8 = 32$. <br> A) 24　　B) 32　　C) 40　　D) 96 | 16. <br><br> B |
| 17. | For choice D, $(2 \times 100) + (9 \times 10) + 14 = 200 + 90 + 14 = 304 \neq 294$. <br> A) $(1 \times 100) + (19 \times 10) + 4$　　B) $(1 \times 100) + (9 \times 10) + 104$ <br> C) $(2 \times 100) + (9 \times 10) + 4$　　D) $(2 \times 100) + (9 \times 10) + 14$ | 17. <br> D |
| 18. | From 778 to 800 is 23 numbers. From 801 to 887 is another 87 numbers. In all, there are $23 + 87 = 110$ numbers. <br> A) 100　　B) 109　　C) 110　　D) 111 | 18. <br> C |
| 19. | $111\ 111 = 11 \times 10101$, so the answer is D. <br> A) 1　　B) 111　　C) 11 111　　D) 111 111 | 19. <br> D |
| 20. | 41 weeks = 287 days; 9 months < 279 days; 1 year ≥ 365 days. <br> A) 288 days　　B) 41 weeks　　C) 9 months　　D) 1 year | 20. <br> A |
| 21. | $5 \times 2 \times 5 \times 2 \times 5 \times 2 \times 5 \times 2 \times 5 \times 2 = 10 \times 10 \times 10 \times 10 \times 10 = 100\ 000$. <br> A) 50　　B) 10 000　　C) 50 000　　D) 100 000 | 21. <br> D |
| 22. | Since half the sum is 20, their sum is 40. If one of the numbers is 7, the other number is $40 - 7 = 33$. <br> A) 3　　B) 13　　C) 26　　D) 33 | 22. <br> D |
| 23. | $(100 \times 5¢) + (100 \times 10¢) + (100 \times 25¢) = 5000¢ + 1000¢ + 2500¢ = 4000¢$. <br> A) $34　　B) $39　　C) $40　　D) $75 | 23. <br> C |
| 24. | $1\frac{1}{5} + 2\frac{2}{5} + 3\frac{3}{5} + 4\frac{4}{5} = 10\frac{10}{5} = 10 + 2 = 12$. <br> A) 6　　B) 10　　C) 12　　D) 13 | 24. <br><br> C |
| 25. | I earned $1 + $2 + $4 + $8 + $16 + $32 + $64 = $127. So the answer is C. <br> A) $63　　B) $64　　C) $127　　D) $128 | 25. <br> C |
| 26. | Since $7^2 - 6^2 = 49 - 36 = 13$, the ones' digit is 3. <br> A) 4　　B) 3　　C) 2　　D) 1 | 26. <br> B |
| 27. | Since each pair of numbers after 10 equals 0, the answer is A. <br> A) 10　　B) 7　　C) 1　　D) 0 | 27. <br> A |
| 28. | $1 \div \frac{1}{2} = 1 \times \frac{2}{1} = 1 \times 2 = 2$. <br> A) $\frac{1}{2}$　　B) 1　　C) $1\frac{1}{2}$　　D) 2 | 28. <br><br> D |
| 29. | The square root of 16 is 4 and the square root of 4 is 2. <br> A) 2　　B) 4　　C) 16　　D) 64 | 29. <br> A |

*Go on to the next page* ⇒ **6**

| | |
|---|---|
| 30. Of the listed numbers, only 2100 is divisible by 2, 3, 4, and 5.<br>   A) 2001       B) 2010       C) 2100       D) 2110 | 30.<br>C |
| 31. Al spent \$12 and Bob spent \$8. Together, Al and Bob spent \$20. Carl spent \$24 − \$20 = \$4. So, the correct answer is A.<br><br>   A) \$4       B) \$6       C) \$8       D) \$20 | 31.<br><br>A |
| 32. Each side of the square is $4 \div 4 = 1$ and the area is $1 \times 1 = 1$.<br>   A) 1       B) 2       C) 4       D) 16 | 32.<br>A |
| 33. $30 \times 40 \times 50 = (3 \times 2 \times 5) \times (2 \times 2 \times 2 \times 5) \times (2 \times 5 \times 5)$.<br>   A) 3       B) 5       C) 10       D) 50 | 33.<br>B |
| 34. If \$100 is increased by 50%, one gets \$150. If \$300 is decreased by 50%, one also gets \$150. So the answer is D.<br>   A) 200%       B) 150%       C) 100%       D) 50% | 34.<br>D |
| 35. Since the sum is a 3-digit number, $A = 1$.<br>Since the sum is 111, $B = 2$ and $C = 9$.<br>The correct answer is B.     $\begin{array}{r} A\,B \\ +\,C\,C \\ \hline A\,A\,A \end{array}$<br>   A) 1       B) 9       C) 8       D) 7 | 35.<br><br>B |
| 36. The largest whole number less than 10 000 whose digits are are all different is 9876. The ones' digit is 6.<br>   A) 6       B) 7       C) 8       D) 9 | 36.<br>A |
| 37. 4 tacs = 6 toes; so 3 tics = 6 toes or $\frac{1}{2}$ tic = 1 toe.<br>   A) $\frac{1}{6}$ tic       B) $\frac{1}{2}$ tic       C) 2 tics       D) 6 tics | 37.<br>B |
| 38. The next *descending* year is 2210. This occurs in the 23rd century.<br><br>   A) 23rd century       B) 24th century<br>   C) 25th century       D) 26th century | 38.<br><br>A |
| 39. A radius of the circle is 6 and a diameter is 12. The smallest surrounding square's side is equal to a diameter. Its area is 144.<br>   A) 18       B) 36       C) 72       D) 144 | 39.<br>D |
| 40. We have 1 1-digit number, 10 2-digit numbers, and 100 3-digit numbers for a total of 321 digits. From 2000 to 2168 is $4 \times 169 = 676$ digits. The next number is 2169 and the *1000th digit* is 6.<br>   A) 6       B) 7       C) 8       D) 9 | 40.<br><br>A |

*The end of the contest* ✍ **6**

## Solutions

# 1987-88 Annual 6th Grade Contest
*Tuesday, March 8, 1988*

**6**

### Contest Information

■ **Solutions** Turn the page for detailed contest solutions (written in the question boxes) and letter answers (in the answer columns on the right).

■ **Scores** When reviewing these questions, remember *this is a contest, not a test*. There is no "passing" or "failing" score. Few students score as high as 30 points (75% correct); students with even half that, 15 points, *deserve commendation!*

■ **Answers & Rating Scale** Turn to page 97 for the letter answers to each question and the rating scale for this contest.

| | |
|---|---|
| 1. Since 26 Vulcons and 45 Clingons were invited on the Inter-prise,there are 45−26=19 more Clingons than Vulcons invited.<br>A) 9      B) 11      C) 19      D) 29 | 1.<br>C |
| 2. 1492 + 1988 + 2001 = 5481, so the correct answer is C.<br>A) 5371      B) 5471      C) 5481      D) 5491 | 2.<br>C |
| 3. $20 \div (10 + 10) = 20 \div 20 = 1$.<br>A) 1      B) 2      C) 10      D) 12 | 3.<br>A |
| 4. $9 + 99 + 999 = 10 + 100 + 1000 - 3 = 1110 - 3 = 1107$.<br>A) 1007      B) 1087      C) 1097      D) 1107 | 4.<br>D |
| 5. The tens' digit of 1988 is 8, which is less than 9.<br>A) ones'      B) hundreds'    C) thousands'   D) ten-thousands' | 5.<br>B |
| 6. $99 \times 78 = (100 \times 78) - (1 \times 78) = 7800 - 78 = 7722$.<br>A) 7612      B) 7622      C) 7712      D) 7722 | 6.<br>D |
| 7. Count July 17 *and* July 31 for a total of $31 - 17 + 1 = 15$ days.<br>A) for 14 days   B) for 15 days   C) for 16 days   D) for 24 days | 7.<br>B |
| 8. $19 \times 88 = 19 \times 2 \times 44 = 38 \times 44$, so A is correct.<br>A) 44      B) 69      C) 88      D) 176 | 8.<br>A |
| 9. 60 min. from now is 12:45 PM; 59 min. from now is 12:44 PM<br>A) 10:46 AM   B) 12:44 AM   C) 12:44 PM   D) 12:46 PM | 9.<br>C |
| 10. The product of 2 and 3 is 6, while the sum of 2 and 3 is 5. So the correct answer is B.<br>A) 1, 2      B) 2, 3      C) 3, 4      D) 4, 5 | 10.<br>B |
| 11. Each row has a sum of 45. Since there are 4 rows, the total is $4 \times 45 = 180$.<br><br>A) 45      B) 49      C) 180      D) 445 | 11.<br>C |
| 12. The sum of the two smallest prime numbers is $2 + 3 = 5 > 3$.<br>A) even                 B) odd<br>C) divisible by 3      D) greater than 3 | 12.<br>D |
| 13. The sum of 10 tens is $10 \times 10 = 100 = 10^2$.<br>A) $10^2$      B) $10^{10}$      C) $10^{100}$      D) $10^{1000}$ | 13.<br>A |
| 14. $509 + 328 = 837$.<br>A) 387      B) 827      C) 837      D) 917 | 14.<br>C |
| 15. Of the years from 1988 through 2001, only 1999 and 2000 have *three* equal digits. The correct answer is choice B.<br>A) 1      B) 2      C) 10      D) 11 | 15.<br>B |
| 16. $225 \div 15 = 15$; no other number listed is divisible by 15.<br>A) 225      B) 425      C) 515      D) 1550 | 16.<br>A |

| | | |
|---|---|---|
| 17. | The next two whole numbers ending in 7 are 27 and 37. Since $27 = 3 \times 9$, it is not prime. But 37 is a prime number.<br>A) 27     B) 37     C) 47     D) 57 | 17.<br>B |
| 18. | $1+1+2+2 \neq$ odd or a multiple of 4; $1+1+1+2 \neq$ even.<br>A) even            B) odd<br>C) a whole number    D) divisible by 4 | 18.<br>C |
| 19. | There are 6 shaded circles and 12 circles in all. Their ratio is 6:12 = 1:2.<br>A) 1:2     B) 1:1     C) 2:1     D) 6:11 | 19.<br>A |
| 20. | If the average of two numbers is 8, their sum is 16. Since their product is 55, the numbers are 5 and 11.<br>A) 5     B) 7     C) 9     D) 11 | 20.<br>D |
| 21. | The ones' digit is 9, so round up to 10; 999 999 increases by 1.<br>A) 999 900    B) 999 990    C) 999 000    D) 1 000 000 | 21.<br>D |
| 22. | $10^3 = 1000$, $10^4 = 10000$, $2^5 = 32$, $2^6 = 64$, $2^9 = 512$, $2^{13} = 8192$.<br>A) $2^5$     B) $2^6$     C) $2^9$     D) $2^{13}$ | 22.<br>D |
| 23. | $2550 = 50 \times 51$, so the correct answer is choice D.<br><br>A) 25     B) 26     C) 50     D) 51 | 23.<br>D |
| 24. | The measure of an angle of a square is 90° and the measure of an angle of an equilateral triangle is 60°. The difference is 30°.<br>A) 30°     B) 45°     C) 60°     D) 90° | 24.<br>A |
| 25. | If 1 bleep = 6 peeps, multiply by 100: 100 bleeps = 600 peeps.<br>A) 10 bleeps   B) 100 bleeps   C) 3600 bleeps   D) 6000 bleeps | 25.<br>B |
| 26. | $6^3 - 5^3 = 216 - 125 = 91$; so last digit is 1 and answer is > 1.<br>A) 1     B) 1951     C) 1973     D) 1987 | 26.<br>B |
| 27. | $4500 \div 250 = 18$, so Joy needs 18 packages.<br><br>A) 9     B) 16     C) 18     D) 20 | 27.<br>C |
| 28. | $\frac{2}{3} + \frac{2}{3} + \frac{2}{3} = \frac{6}{3} = 2$, so choice D is correct.<br>A) 1     B) $1\frac{1}{3}$     C) $1\frac{2}{3}$     D) 2 | 28.<br>D |
| 29. | Red pens are sold at 3 for $1 and black pens are sold at 4 for $1.50. So 12 red pens cost $4 \times \$1 = \$4$ and 24 black pens cost $6 \times \$1.50 = \$9.00$ for a total $13. Her change is $20 - $13 = $7.<br>A) $7     B) $9     C) $13     D) $16 | 29.<br>A |
| 30. | Area of a square is $s^2$. The sides are whole numbers, so the area is a perfect square. Since $400 = 20 \times 20$, choice C is correct.<br>A) 200 cm$^2$    B) 300 cm$^2$    C) 400 cm$^2$    D) 500 cm$^2$ | 30.<br>C |

| | |
|---|---|
| 31. 365 days is one full year, so the date is March 2, 1989.<br>A) March 1     B) March 2     C) March 3     D) March 4 | 31.<br>B |

32. $CD + EF = AB$ and $DE + FA = BC$.
The perimeter of $ABCDEF =$
$AB + BC + CD + EF + DE + FA$
$= AB + BC + AB + BC = 20 + 15$
$+ 20 + 15 = 70$.

A) 35          B) 70          C) 75          D) 80

32.

B

33. 12 of the 1st 25 positive integers are even. If 5 even numbers are removed, 7 of the remaining 20 numbers (35%) are even.

A) 20%          B) 25%          C) 28%          D) 35%

33.
D

34. Since Steve answered 10 questions, he left 10 unanswered. His score was $5 \times 5 + 10 \times 2 + 5 \times 0 = 25 + 20 = 45$.

A) 25          B) 45          C) 50          D) 55

34.

B

35. Work from the inner square to the outer square. Removing the inner square first, $\boxed{\boxed{4}} = \boxed{16} = 16 \times 16 = 256$.

A) 256          B) 128          C) 64          D) 16

35.
A

36. The 4th, 8th, 12th, . . . , 1980th, 1984th, and 1988th letters of $ABCDABCDABCD$ . . . are all $D$'s.

A) $A$          B) $B$          C) $C$          D) $D$

36.
D

37. Area of one circle is $36\pi$; radius
$= 6$. Since $AB$ is equal to a diameter
and $AD$ is twice a diameter, area of
$ABCD = 12 \times 24 = 288$.

A) 72          B) 144          C) 288          D) 576

37.

C

38. The product is greater than $10 \times 10 \times 10 \times 11 = 11\ 000$ and less than $100 \times 100 \times 100 \times 99 = 99\ 000\ 000$. So choice C is correct.

A) 6561          B) 10 001          C) 28 101 810     D) 99 999 999

38.
C

39. The difference in the rates of the two cars is 10 km/hr. In one hour, the faster car will gain 10 km on the slower car. In half an hour, the faster car will gain 5 km. So it takes the faster car 1½ hours = 90 minutes to catch up to the slower car.

A) 60 minutes  B) 75 minutes  C) 80 minutes  D) 90 minutes

39.

D

40. The factors may be written as 8 pairs, each pair having a product of 1000. The product of all factors is $1000^8 = 10^{24}$.

A) $10^8$          B) $10^{16}$          C) $10^{24}$          D) $10^{32}$

40.
C

*The end of the contest* ✍️     **6**

# 1988-89 Annual 6th Grade Contest

*Tuesday, March 14, 1989*

**6**

## Contest Information

- **Solutions** Turn the page for detailed contest solutions (written in the question boxes) and letter answers (in the answer columns on the right).

- **Scores** When reviewing these questions, remember *this is a contest, not a test*. There is no "passing" or "failing" score. Few students score as high as 30 points (75% correct); students with even half that, 15 points, *deserve commendation!*

- **Answers & Rating Scale** Turn to page 98 for the letter answers to each question and the rating scale for this contest.

| | |
|---|---|
| 1. Since the numbers are equal and nonzero, the quotient is 1.<br>A) 0          B) 1          C) 2          D) 1989 | 1.<br>B |
| 2. The insect collector caught 123 + 234 + 345 = 702 insects, so the correct answer is D.<br>A) 456 insects  B) 678 insects  C) 602 insects  D) 702 insects | 2.<br>D |
| 3. 3223 − 1989 = (3223 − 2000) + 11 = 1223 + 11 = 1234.<br>A) 2234          B) 1324          C) 1234          D) 1144 | 3.<br>C |
| 4. 1 minute = 60 seconds, so 6 minutes = 6×60 seconds = 360.<br>A) 10          B) 36          C) 60          D) 360 | 4.<br>D |
| 5. 100 × 99 × 100 = (100 × 99) × 100 = 9900 × 100.<br>A) 10          B) 100          C) 1000          D) 9900 | 5.<br>B |
| 6. 1×9×9×0  = 0; from the others, choose the largest last digit.<br>A) 1×9×8×7  B) 1×9×8×8  C) 1×9×8×9  D) 1×9×9×0 | 6.<br>C |
| 7. 10 101+99 999 = (10 101+100 000) − 1 = 110 101 − 1 = 110 100.<br>A) 19 191          B) 101 010          C) 110 100          D) 119 191 | 7.<br>C |
| 8. 18 = 6×3 & 30 = 6×5; least common multiple = 6×3×5 = 90.<br>A) 90          B) 18          C) 12          D) 6 | 8.<br>A |
| 9. (123×456) − (123×455) = 123×(456 − 455) = 123×1 = 123.<br>A) 456          B) 455          C) 123          D) 1 | 9.<br>C |
| 10. Increase the hundredths' digit by 1: 9.89 + 0.01 = 9.90.<br>A) 9.89          B) 9.90          C) 9.99          D) 10.00 | 10.<br>B |
| 11. 2×4×5×6 = 2×4×5×(2×3) = (2×4×2)×5×3 = 16×15.<br>A) 4          B) 6          C) 8          D) 16 | 11.<br>D |
| 12. The tens' digit of 1989 is 8 and the hundreds' digit is 4. Since 8 − 4 = 4, the correct answer is choice B.<br>A) 1          B) 4          C) 5          D) 6 | 12.<br>B |
| 13. Since 48+49+50+51+52 = 200+50, the missing number is 50.<br>A) 0          B) 4          C) 46          D) 50 | 13.<br>D |
| 14. The square is divided into 4 triangles of equal area. Each of the 3 shaded triangles has an area of 24÷3 = 8, so the area of the square is 4×8 = 32.<br>A) 8          B) 32          C) 48          D) 96 | 14.<br>B |
| 15. If Ronald ate 1 sandwich, Mickey Moose ate 2, for a total of 3. If Ronald ate 2 sandwiches, Mickey ate 4, for a total of 6.<br>A) 4          B) 3          C) 2          D) 1 | 15.<br>C |

*Go on to the next page* ▌▶   **6**

| | |
|---|---|
| 16. 1 000 000 + 1 000 = 1 001 000, so choice A is correct.<br>A) 1 001 000    B) 1 000 100    C) 101 000    D) 100 100 | 16.<br>A |
| 17. 2 + 3 + 5 + 7 + 11 = 28. (Note: 1 is *not* prime.)<br>A) 28    B) 26    C) 18    D) 17 | 17.<br>A |
| 18. $22 000 000÷100 = $220 000. Since the fight lasted 91 seconds rather than 100, his actual earnings per second was a bit more.<br>A) $2 400    B) $24 000    C) $240 000    D) $2 400 000 | 18.<br>C |
| 19. The factors of 28 are 1, 2, 4, 7, and 14; their sum is 28.<br>A) 11    B) 12    C) 14    D) 28 | 19.<br>D |
| 20. The cost for 1 year (52 weeks) is 52×60¢ = $31.20. The cost, to the nearest $10, was $30.<br>A) $300    B) $60    C) $30    D) $10 | 20.<br>C |
| 21. This equals 247×(1000+100+10+1) = 247×1111 = 247×11×101.<br>A) 2    B) 3    C) 4    D) 11 | 21.<br>D |
| 22. If the square of the perimeter of a square is 400, the perimeter is 20 and each side is 20÷4 = 5. Its area is 5×5 = 25.<br>A) 5    B) 25    C) 100    D) 400 | 22.<br>B |
| 23. 1000 bees take 2 year to make 7 jars of honey; so it takes 1000 bees 20 years to make 70 jars. 5000 bees take 20÷5 = 4 years.<br>A) 2 years    B) 4 years    C) 5 years    D) 7 years | 23.<br>B |
| 24. 2 + 2 + 2 + 2 + 2 + 2 + 2 + 2 = 16, so choice B is correct.<br>A) $2^3$    B) $2^4$    C) $2^8$    D) $2^{16}$ | 24.<br>B |
| 25. The perimeter (circumference) of the semi-circle = $\pi r$ = $5\pi$. The perimeter of the entire region (including the diameter) is $5\pi$ + 10.<br>A) $5\pi$    B) $10\pi$    C) $5\pi$ + 10    D) $10\pi$ + 10 | 25.<br>C |
| 26. (3 × 4 × 5) + (3 × 4 × 6) = (3 × 4) × (5 + 6) = (3 × 4) × 11 = (3 × 4) × (10 + 1) = (3 × 4 × 10) + (3 × 4 × 1).<br>A) 1    B) 3    C) 20    D) 21 | 26.<br>A |
| 27. The sum of the measures of all 3 angles is 180°; the sum of the measures of the 2 equal angles is 60°. Each has measure 30°.<br>A) 20°    B) 30°    C) 40°    D) 60° | 27.<br>B |
| 28. 1 hour 42 minutes + 6 hours 59 minutes + 6 hours 13 minutes = 13 hours 114 minutes = 14 hours 54 minutes; 12 hours from 9 A.M. is 9 P.M. and 2 hours 54 minutes later is 11:54 P.M..<br>A) 10:54 P.M.    B) 11:54 P.M.    C) 12:54 P.M.    D) 1:54 A.M. | 28.<br>B |
| 29. If a whole number greater than 1 is divisible only by 1 and itself, the number is always prime.<br>A) even    B) odd    C) a square    D) a prime | 29.<br>D |

| | | |
|---|---|---|
| 30. | At the end of the 1st day, I have $1 + $3 = $4. At the end of the 2nd day, I have $4+ 3×$4 = $16. At the end of the 3rd day, I have $16 + 3×$16 = $64. The correct answer is choice D <br><br> A) $27      B) $28      C) $49      D) $64 | 30. <br><br> D |
| 31. | Solve the proportion 10:15 = 6: ? . This is equivalent to 2:3 = 6: ? . Since 2:3 = 6:9, shadow is 9 m long. <br> A) 11 m    B) 10 m    C) 9 m    D) 8 m | 31. <br> C |
| 32. | Circumference of front wheel is twice that of rear wheel. So the rear wheel must revolve twice as often as front wheel. <br> A) once    B) twice    C) 4 times    D) 8 times | 32. <br> C |
| 33. | The average of an odd number of consecutive integers is the middle number. So the largest is 10 more than 31, namely 41. <br> A) 40      B) 41      C) 51      D) 52 | 33. <br> B |
| 34. | An integer which is divisible by 5, 6, 8, and 9 must also be be divisible by their least common multiple; their LCM is 360. <br> A) 28      B) 360      C) 720      D) 5689 | 34. <br> B |
| 35. | The four small triangles can be rearranged to fill up the smaller square, so the sum of the area of the four triangles equals the area of the small square. It's area is half the area of the big square, and 100 ÷ 2 = 50. <br> A) 80      B) 75      C) 50      D) 10 | 35. <br><br> C |
| 36. | Consonant to letter ratio is 5:8. There are 5×1200 =6000 letters; 5 of every 8 are consonants. So, (6000÷8)×5 are consonants. <br> A) 2250    B) 3600    C) 3750    D) 10 000 | 36. <br> C |
| 37. | The cat runs at 6 m per second, so it gains 4 m on the mouse each second and will need 12÷4 = 3 seconds to gain 12 m. <br> A) 2 seconds   B) 3 seconds   C) 4 seconds   D) 6 seconds | 37. <br> B |
| 38. | There are 2 sides with 1988 dots and 2 sides with 1989 dots, for a total of 7954 dots. But each corner has been counted twice. Since there are 4 corners, the total number of dots on the outside is 7954 − 4 = 7950. <br><br> A) 7950     B) 7952     C) 7954     D) 7956 | 38. <br><br> A |
| 39. | The 4th, 8th, 12th, . . . , 1980th, 1984th, and 1988th letters are all *H*'s. So the 1989th letter is an *M*. <br> A) *A*      B) *T*      C) *H*      D) *M* | 39. <br> D |
| 40. | The digits from 1 to 9 have a sum of 45, so the ones' digit is 5. Since this sum is taken 100 000 times, the ones' digit is 0. <br> A) 0      B) 1      C) 5      D) 9 | 40. <br> A |

*The end of the contest* ✍🏻 **6**

## Solutions

# 1989-90 Annual 6th Grade Contest
*Tuesday, March 13, 1990*

# 6

## Contest Information

- **Solutions** Turn the page for detailed contest solutions (written in the question boxes) and letter answers (in the answer columns on the right).

- **Scores** When reviewing these questions, remember *this is a contest, not a test*. There is no "passing" or "failing" score. Few students score as high as 30 points (75% correct); students with even half that, 15 points, *deserve commendation!*

- **Answers & Rating Scale** Turn to page 99 for the letter answers to each question and the rating scale for this contest.

| | | |
|---|---|---|
| 1. | $(1 + 9) \times (9 + 0) = (10) \times (9) = 90.$ <br> A) 0     B) 10     C) 90     D) 1990 | 1. <br> C |
| 2. | 20 nickels $= 20 \times 5¢ = 100¢.$ <br> A) 5 dimes    B) 100 pennies   C) 5 quarters   D) 2 dollars | 2. <br> B |
| 3. | $9898 - 8989 = 909.$ <br> A) 89     B) 909     C) 989     D) 1010 | 3. <br> B |
| 4. | Catman can park for four 20-minute periods. <br><br> A) 4 minutes   B) 5 minutes    C) 60 minutes   D) 80 minutes | 4. <br> D |
| 5. | $10 \times 10 < 113 < 11 \times 11$, so the answer is B. <br> A) 9 and 10    B) 10 and 11    C) 56 and 57    D) 112 and 114 | 5. <br> B |
| 6. | In the word *mathematics*, there are 4 vowels and 7 consonants, so the ratio sought is 4:7. <br> A) 4:7     B) 7:4     C) 4:11     D) 7:11 | 6. <br> A |
| 7. | $7 \div 7 \times 7 = (7 \div 7) \times 7 = 1 \times 7 = 7.$ [Note: This is problem #7.] <br> A) 0     B) $1 \div 7$     C) 1     D) 7 | 7. <br> D |
| 8. | $1 \text{ m} - 1 \text{ cm} = 100 \text{ cm} - 1 \text{ cm} = 99 \text{ cm.}$ <br> A) 99 cm     B) 9 cm     C) 99 m     D) 9 m | 8. <br> A |
| 9. | $(1 \times 10^3) + (9 \times 10^2) + (9 \times 10^1) = 1000 + 900 + 90.$ <br> A) 199     B) 1990     C) 19900     D) 81000 | 9. <br> B |
| 10. | If, when an even prime number is subtracted from an odd prime, the result is 1, the subtraction must be $3-2 = 1.$ <br> A) 1     B) 2     C) 3     D) 5 | 10. <br> C |
| 11. | Rewrite as $(20 \div 40) \times (20 \div 40) \times (20 \div 40) = 0.5 \times 0.5 \times 0.5 = 0.125.$ <br> A) 0.125     B) 0.25     C) 0.5     D) 2 | 11. <br> A |
| 12. | 4 hours 55 mins. + 2 hours 48 mins. = 7 hours 43 mins. <br> A) 2, 7     B) 7, 3     C) 7, 33     D) 7, 43 | 12. <br> D |
| 13. | $13 + 14 + 15 + 16 + 17 = 75 = 15 \times 5.$ <br> A) 3     B) 5     C) 15     D) 17 | 13. <br> B |
| 14. | Each side can cross the circle at most twice, and $3 \times 2 = 6.$ <br> A) 6 points    B) 5 points    C) 4 points    D) 3 points | 14. <br> A |
| 15. | 31 days is 4 weeks + 3 days, so it's 3 days from a Tuesday! <br> A) Tuesday    B) Wednesday   C) Thursday    D) Friday | 15. <br> D |

*Go on to the next page* ⦀➡ **6**

| | | | | | |
|---|---|---|---|---|---|
| 16. | The whole number factors of 16 are 1, 2, 4, 8, and 16. | | | | 16. |
| | A) 2 | B) 4 | C) 5 | D) 8 | C |
| 17. | If I answer only 10 questions correctly, then, for the remaining 30 questions, *75% of the total*, I'd be marked *wrong*. | | | | 17. |
| | A) 25% | B) 30% | C) 40% | D) 75% | D |
| 18. | $256 - 128 = 128$, so the answer is choice C. | | | | 18. |
| | A) $2^5$ | B) $2^6$ | C) $2^7$ | D) $2^8$ | C |
| 19. | If two numbers have a sum of 12 and a difference of 2, the two numbers are 7 and 5, so their product is 35. | | | | 19. |
| | A) 35 | B) 24 | C) 14 | D) 6 | A |
| 20. | Count by 10's: 19–28, 29–38, . . . , 79–88. Now count 89 & 90. | | | | 20. |
| | A) 70 tickets | B) 71 tickets | C) 72 tickets | D) 109 tickets | C |
| 21. | One swing in 2 seconds is 30 swings each minute. That's a total of $60 \times 30 = 1800$ swings each hour. | | | | 21. |
| | A) 30 | B) 1800 | C) 3600 | D) 7200 | B |
| 22. | $10 \times 20 \times 30 = 10 \times (2 \times 10) \times (3 \times 10) = (2 \times 3) \times (10 \times 10 \times 10)$. | | | | 22. |
| | A) 6 | B) 60 | C) 600 | D) 6000 | A |
| 23. | Choice A = 1, B = 8, C = 9, and D = 4. The largest is C. | | | | 23. |
| | A) $1^4$ | B) $2^3$ | C) $3^2$ | D) $4^1$ | C |
| 24. | If the perimeter is 48, each side is 12 and the area is 144. | | | | 24. |
| | A) 192 | B) 144 | C) 48 | D) 36 | B |
| 25. | If I get a penny the 1st day and a nickel the 2nd, I get 6¢ every 2 days. In 20 days, I'd get 60¢. | | | | 25. |
| | A) 20¢ | B) 30¢ | C) 60¢ | D) $1.20 | C |
| 26. | $(7+8+9) + (7+8+9) + (7+8+9) - (7+8+9)$ is choice B. | | | | 26. |
| | A) $1 \times (7+8+9)$ | B) $2 \times (7+8+9)$ | C) $3 \times (7+8+9)$ | D) $4 \times (7+8+9)$ | B |
| 27. | The side is more than $10-4 = 6$ and less than $10+4 = 14$. | | | | 27. |
| | A) 1 | B) 4 | C) 6 | D) 13 | D |
| 28. | John gave $160 to his brother. Of the remaining $240, he spent 10%, or $24. This left John with $240 - $24 = $216. | | | | 28. |
| | A) $200 | B) $216 | C) $240 | D) $350 | B |
| 29. | If the largest angle equals the sum of the other two angles, then the largest angle is half of 180°, so it must be 90°. | | | | 29. |
| | A) 30° | B) 45° | C) 60° | D) 90° | D |

*Go on to the next page* ⫸  **6**

| | | |
|---|---|---|
| 30. | My cost is $6 \times \$1 + 8 \times \$15 = \$6 + \$120 = \$126$. My average cost per tape is $\$126 \div 14 = \$9.00$<br>A) \$7.50          B) \$8.00          C) \$9.00          D) \$12.00 | 30.<br>C |
| 31. | By definition of *prime*, the product of primes is not prime.<br>A) positive     B) odd          C) even          D) prime | 31.<br>D |
| 32. | Since A = $\pi r^2$, $r = 1$. Since C = $2\pi r$, the circumference is $2\pi$.<br>A) 1               B) $\pi$               C) $2\pi$               D) $4\pi$ | 32.<br>C |
| 33. | Choice A has 10 zeroes, B has 12, C has 12, and D has 6.<br>A) $100^5$          B) $1000^4$          C) $10000^3$          D) 1 million | 33.<br>A |
| 34. | The factors 5, 10, 20 make the number a multiple of 1000.<br>A) 0               B) 1               C) 2               D) 5 | 34.<br>A |
| 35. | The wheels move the same distance, so the bigger wheel makes fewer turns. The distance covered by 12 front wheel turns equals that of 10 rear wheel turns. The answer is B.<br>A) 96 times     B) 100 times     C) 120 times     D) 144 times | 35.<br>B |
| 36. | 1.9 hours is 1 hour and 54 minutes, so the answer is C.<br>A) 1:13 P.M.     B) 1:54 P.M.     C) 1:58 P.M.     D) 2:00 P.M. | 36.<br>C |
| 37. | By trial, only $0 \times 1$, $1 \times 2$, $1 \times 2 \times 3$ (or $2 \times 3$), $1 \times 2 \times 3 \times 4$ (or $2 \times 3 \times 4$), $3 \times 4$, $4 \times 5$, $5 \times 6$, and $6 \times 7$ qualify—that's 8 *values*.<br>A) 25               B) 8               C) 7               D) 6 | 37.<br>B |
| 38. | Each shaded region is congruent to the unshaded region directly across from it, so the shaded area is just half the total area.<br>A) $6\pi$          B) $12\pi$          C) $18\pi$          D) $36\pi$ | 38.<br>C |
| 39. | Insert the digit "1" between the two digits of each of the 90 numbers from 10 to 99—and you'll produce all the numbers!<br>A) 89               B) 90               C) 99               D) 100 | 39.<br>B |
| 40. | Only 5 odds (whose sum is odd) and 10 evens (whose sum is even) remain. Their sum must be odd + even, or odd.<br>A) 163          B) 168          C) 186          D) 196 | 40.<br>A |

*The end of the contest* ✍     **6**

# Solutions

## 1990-91 Annual 6th Grade Contest

*Tuesday, March 12, 1991*

**6**

### Contest Information

- **Solutions** Turn the page for detailed contest solutions (written in the question boxes) and letter answers (in the answer columns on the right).

- **Scores** When reviewing these questions, remember *this is a contest, not a test*. There is no "passing" or "failing" score. Few students score as high as 30 points (75% correct); students with even half that, 15 points, *deserve commendation!*

- **Answers & Rating Scale** Turn to page 100 for the letter answers to each question and the rating scale for this contest.

| | | |
|---|---|---|
| 1. | $(1 + 1) \times (1 + 1) \times (1 + 1) = 2 \times 2 \times 2 = 8.$ <br> A) 8  B) 6  C) 4  D) 1 | 1. <br> A |
| 2. | If I eat 3 meals each day, I eat $3 \times 7 = 21$ meals each week. <br> A) 3  B) 7  C) 15  D) 21 | 2. <br> D |
| 3. | $11+22+33+44 = 11 \times (1+2+3+4) = 11 \times 10 = 110.$ <br> A) 90  B) 100  C) 109  D) 110 | 3. <br> D |
| 4. | If two numbers have a sum of 4 and a difference of 4, the numbers must be 0 and 4, so their product is 0. <br> A) 0  B) 4  C) 8  D) 16 | 4. <br> A |
| 5. | $(1 \div 1) + (2 \div 2) + (3 \div 3) = 1 + 1 + 1 = 3.$ <br> A) 1  B) 3  C) 4  D) 6 | 5. <br> B |
| 6. | $4 \div 4 = 1$, which is an odd number. <br> A) $4 + 4$  B) $4 - 4$  C) $4 \times 4$  D) $4 \div 4$ | 6. <br> D |
| 7. | $1 \times 11 \times 111 = 11 \times 111 = 1221.$ <br> A) 1111  B) 1221  C) 1331  D) 1441 | 7. <br> B |
| 8. | Since $24 = 4 \times 6$ and $42 = 7 \times 6$, the greatest common factor is 6. <br> A) 6  B) 8  C) 12  D) 24 | 8. <br> A |
| 9. | The four factors are 1, 2, 3, and 6 – and their sum is 12. <br> A) $1 \times 6$  B) $2 \times 6$  C) $3 \times 6$  D) $4 \times 6$ | 9. <br> B |
| 10. | The square is greater than $6^2$ and less than $8^2$, so the square is $7^2$ and the whole number is 7. <br> A) 5  B) 6  C) 7  D) 8 | 10. <br> C |
| 11. | 1991 divided by 11 equals 181. Check it with a calculator. <br> A) 161  B) 171  C) 181  D) 191 | 11. <br> C |
| 12. | Since $A = 16$, $B = 27$, $C = 16$, and $D = 24$, the answer is B. <br> A) $2 \times 2 \times 2 \times 2$  B) $3 \times 3 \times 3$  C) $4 \times 4$  D) $2 \times 3 \times 4$ | 12. <br> B |
| 13. | The *even* integers greater than 0 and less than 1000 together with the *odd* integers greater than 0 and less than 1000 make up the integers from 1 through 999. <br> A) 499  B) 500  C) 999  D) 1000 | 13. <br> C |
| 14. | $144 = 16 \times 9 = 2^4 \times 3^2.$ <br> A) $2^4 \times 3^2$  B) $2^5 \times 3^1$  C) $2^3 \times 3^3$  D) $2^2 \times 3^4$ | 14. <br> A |
| 15. | $121212 \div 12 = (120000 + 1200 + 12) \div 12 = 10000 + 100 + 1 = 10101.$ <br> A) 111  B) 1001  C) 1212  D) 10101 | 15. <br> D |

*Go on to the next page* ⫸ **6**

| | | |
|---|---|---|
| 16. | The average of three consecutive integers is the middle one.<br>A) 1991        B) 1992        C) 1993        D) 5973 | 16.<br>A |
| 17. | In the diagram at the right, the length of a side of one square is 6, so $AB = CD = 6$ and $BC = AD = 2AF = 2(6) = 12$. Adding, the perimeter of rectangle $ABCD$ is 36.<br>A) 36        B) 40        C) 48        D) 96 | 17.<br><br>A |
| 18. | $1111 - 1001 = 110$.<br>A) 11        B) 110        C) 111        D) 1100 | 18.<br>B |
| 19. | With 4 quarters in \$1, in \$25, there are $4 \times 25 = 100$ quarters<br>A) 10        B) 25        C) 100        D) 500 | 19.<br>C |
| 20. | $\sqrt{4} \times \sqrt{4} \times \sqrt{4} \times \sqrt{4} = 2 \times 2 \times 2 \times 2 = 16$.<br>A) 4        B) 8        C) 16        D) 32 | 20.<br>C |
| 21. | I am 10 years older than my brother. Ten years ago, he was 10. Now he is 20. Now, I am $20+10 = 30$. In 10 years, I'll be 40.<br>A) 10        B) 20        C) 30        D) 40 | 21.<br>D |
| 22. | $6^2 \times 10^2 = 36 \times 100$, and $3600 \div 16 = 225 = 15^2$.<br>A) $3^2$        B) $5^2$        C) $15^2$        D) $30^2$ | 22.<br>C |
| 23. | 100% of 200% equals $1 \times 200\% = 200\%$.<br>A) 20%        B) 200%        C) 2000%        D) 20000% | 23.<br>B |
| 24. | Since $123 \times 456 > 100 \times 456 > 45000$, the answer is D.<br>A) 4000        B) 5000        C) 40000        D) 50000 | 24.<br>D |
| 25. | $(1 \times 2 \times 3 \times 4 \times 5) \div (1+2+3+4+5) = 120 \div 15 = 8$.<br>A) 1        B) 5        C) 8        D) 12 | 25.<br>C |
| 26. | The sum is 10. The product gets smaller as the numbers get further apart. The least product is $1 \times 9 = 9$.<br>A) 0        B) 1        C) 9        D) 10 | 26.<br>C |
| 27. | Points $A$, $B$, $C$, and $D$ lie on a line. If $AD = 30$, and $AC = 20$, then $CD = 10$. No other information is needed.<br>A) 5        B) 10        C) 15        D) 20 | 27.<br><br>B |
| 28. | The only prime divisible by 13 is 13.<br>A) 0        B) 1        C) 2        D) 13 | 28.<br>B |
| 29. | If 14 days (2 weeks) ago was a Tuesday, then today is Tuesday and 14 days from today will still be a Tuesday.<br>A) Tuesday        B) Wednesday   C) Thursday        D) Friday | 29.<br>A |

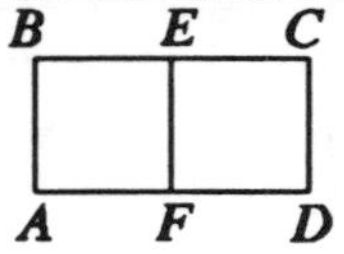

| | | |
|---|---|---|
| 30. | If the sum of the digits is divisible by 9, so is the number. | 30. |
| | A) 333      B) 444      C) 777      D) 888 | A |

| | | |
|---|---|---|
| 31. | $10 \times 100 \times 1000 = 1000 \times 1000 = 1\,000\,000 = 10^6$. | 31. |
| | A) $10^6$      B) $10^7$      C) $10^8$      D) $10^9$ | A |

| | | |
|---|---|---|
| 32. | The remainder is 9876 – 6789 = 3087. | 32. |
| | A) 0      B) 1      C) 1111      D) 3087 | D |

| | | |
|---|---|---|
| 33. | If the product of two consecutive whole numbers is 9900, the numbers are 99 and 100 and their sum is 199. | 33. B |
| | A) 19      B) 199      C) 1109      D) 9901 | |

| | | |
|---|---|---|
| 34. | I have twice as much money as my brother. If I have $10 more than he does, he has $10. Thus, I have $20. | 34. D |
| | A) $5      B) $10      C) $15      D) $20 | |

| | | |
|---|---|---|
| 35. | The perimeter of the larger square is 36, so its side is 9 and its area is $81 = 9^2$. Similarly, a side of the smaller square is 4, and its area is 16. The shaded area is 81 – 16 = 65. | 35. D |
| | A) 4      B) 20      C) 25      D) 65 | |

| | | |
|---|---|---|
| 36. | There are exactly 15 prime numbers less than 50. Between 50 60, the only additional primes are 53 and 59. | 36. C |
| | A) 19      B) 18      C) 17      D) 16 | |

| | | |
|---|---|---|
| 37. | When the number is rounded, the rounded number is at most 50 more than the original number. Since it is twice the the original number, the original number was 50. | 37. B |
| | A) 25      B) 50      C) 100      D) 150 | |

| | | |
|---|---|---|
| 38. | The sum of *all* of the first ten positive whole numbers is 55. Since the given sum was 50, I didn't add the 5. | 38. C |
| | A) 1      B) 3      C) 5      D) 7 | |

| | | |
|---|---|---|
| 39. | (2–1) + (4–3) + (6–5) + . . . + (98–97) + (100–99) = 50. | 39. |
| | A) 1      B) 49      C) 50      D) 100 | C |

| | | |
|---|---|---|
| 40. | Suppose the bottom of the box is $10 \times 8$. Into this I can fit four $5 \times 4$ blocks. But, the $5 \times 4$ blocks are only 2 cm high, so I use get three layers of these blocks, and $3 \times 4 = 12$. | 40. B |
| | A) 10      B) 12      C) 20      D) 60 | |

*The end of the contest* ✍ **6**

# Answers & Ratings

# ANSWERS 1988-89 4TH GRADE CONTEST

| | | | | |
|---|---|---|---|---|
| 1. C | 7. C | 13. C | 19. A | 25. C |
| 2. B | 8. D | 14. B | 20. A | 26. D |
| 3. A | 9. D | 15. C | 21. B | 27. A |
| 4. D | 10. A | 16. A | 22. B | 28. D |
| 5. C | 11. B | 17. D | 23. B | 29. C |
| 6. C | 12. A | 18. C | 24. C | 30. B |

# RATE YOURSELF!!!
## for the 1988-89 4TH GRADE CONTEST

| Score | Rating |
|---|---|
| 27-30 | Another Einstein |
| 24-26 | Mathematical Wizard |
| 22-23 | School Champion |
| 20-21 | Grade Level Champion |
| 17-19 | Best In The Class |
| 14-16 | Excellent Student |
| 11-13 | Good Student |
| 9-10 | Average Student |
| 0-8 | Better Luck Next Time |

# ANSWERS 1989-90 4TH GRADE CONTEST

| | | | | |
|---|---|---|---|---|
| 1. B | 7. D | 13. C | 19. B | 25. C |
| 2. A | 8. C | 14. D | 20. C | 26. D |
| 3. C | 9. A | 15. C | 21. C | 27. B |
| 4. A | 10. C | 16. D | 22. B | 28. A |
| 5. D | 11. B | 17. B | 23. A | 29. A |
| 6. D | 12. A | 18. C | 24. D | 30. B |

# RATE YOURSELF!!!
## for the 1989-90 4th GRADE CONTEST

| Score | Rating |
|---|---|
| 28-30 | Another Einstein |
| 25-27 | Mathematical Wizard |
| 22-24 | School Champion |
| 20-21 | Grade Level Champion |
| 17-19 | Best In The Class |
| 15-16 | Excellent Student |
| 13-14 | Good Student |
| 10-12 | Average Student |
| 0-9 | Better Luck Next Time |

## ANSWERS 1990-91 4TH GRADE CONTEST

| | | | | |
|---|---|---|---|---|
| 1. C | 7. D | 13. D | 19. D | 25. B |
| 2. A | 8. B | 14. B | 20. B | 26. C |
| 3. D | 9. C | 15. A | 21. C | 27. D |
| 4. C | 10. A | 16. B | 22. B | 28. A |
| 5. D | 11. D | 17. D | 23. A | 29. A |
| 6. A | 12. C | 18. B | 24. B | 30. C |

# RATE YOURSELF!!!
## for the 1990-91 4TH GRADE CONTEST

| Score | Rating |
|---|---|
| 28-30 | Another Einstein |
| 26-27 | Mathematical Wizard |
| 23-25 | School Champion |
| 21-22 | Grade Level Champion |
| 18-20 | Best In The Class |
| 15-17 | Excellent Student |
| 13-14 | Good Student |
| 11-12 | Average Student |
| 0-10 | Better Luck Next Time |

## ANSWERS 1988-89 5TH GRADE CONTEST

| | | | | |
|---|---|---|---|---|
| 1. D | 7. D | 13. A | 19. C | 25. C |
| 2. A | 8. D | 14. B | 20. B | 26. B |
| 3. A | 9. C | 15. D | 21. B | 27. C |
| 4. D | 10. C | 16. D | 22. B | 28. C |
| 5. B | 11. C | 17. B | 23. D | 29. A |
| 6. C | 12. C | 18. B | 24. D | 30. A |

# RATE YOURSELF!!!
## for the 1988-89 5TH GRADE CONTEST

| Score | Rating |
|---|---|
| 26-30 | Another Einstein |
| 23-25 | Mathematical Wizard |
| 21-22 | School Champion |
| 18-20 | Grade Level Champion |
| 16-17 | Best In The Class |
| 13-15 | Excellent Student |
| 11-12 | Good Student |
| 9-10 | Average Student |
| 0-8 | Better Luck Next Time |

## ANSWERS 1989-90 5TH GRADE CONTEST

| | | | | |
|---|---|---|---|---|
| 1. B | 7. B | 13. A | 19. C | 25. C |
| 2. B | 8. C | 14. C | 20. B | 26. A |
| 3. A | 9. C | 15. B | 21. D | 27. B |
| 4. C | 10. D | 16. D | 22. D | 28. A |
| 5. B | 11. A | 17. A | 23. B | 29. D |
| 6. C | 12. D | 18. A | 24. A | 30. D |

# RATE YOURSELF!!!
## for the 1989-90 5TH GRADE CONTEST

| Score | Rating |
|---|---|
| 27-30 | Another Einstein |
| 25-26 | Mathematical Wizard |
| 22-24 | School Champion |
| 19-21 | Grade Level Champion |
| 17-18 | Best In The Class |
| 14-16 | Excellent Student |
| 12-13 | Good Student |
| 10-11 | Average Student |
| 0-9 | Better Luck Next Time |

## ANSWERS 1990-91 5TH GRADE CONTEST

| | | | | |
|---|---|---|---|---|
| 1. B | 7. B | 13. C | 19. D | 25. C |
| 2. A | 8. B | 14. B | 20. A | 26. B |
| 3. C | 9. B | 15. B | 21. D | 27. A |
| 4. D | 10. D | 16. D | 22. A | 28. A |
| 5. C | 11. C | 17. A | 23. C | 29. C |
| 6. A | 12. B | 18. D | 24. D | 30. C |

# RATE YOURSELF!!!
### for the 1990-91 5TH GRADE CONTEST

| Score | Rating |
|---|---|
| 28-30 | Another Einstein |
| 25-27 | Mathematical Wizard |
| 23-24 | School Champion |
| 21-22 | Grade Level Champion |
| 19-20 | Best In The Class |
| 16-18 | Excellent Student |
| 13-15 | Good Student |
| 11-12 | Average Student |
| 0-10 | Better Luck Next Time |

## ANSWERS 1986-87 6TH GRADE CONTEST

| | | | | |
|---|---|---|---|---|
| 1. B | 9. A | 17. D | 25. C | 33. B |
| 2. D | 10. A | 18. C | 26. B | 34. D |
| 3. C | 11. C | 19. D | 27. A | 35. B |
| 4. A | 12. C | 20. A | 28. D | 36. A |
| 5. B | 13. C | 21. D | 29. A | 37. B |
| 6. B | 14. B | 22. D | 30. C | 38. A |
| 7. D | 15. A | 23. C | 31. A | 39. D |
| 8. B | 16. B | 24. C | 32. A | 40. A |

# RATE YOURSELF!!!
## for the 1986-87 6TH GRADE CONTEST

| Score | Rating |
|---|---|
| 37-40 | Another Einstein |
| 34-36 | Mathematical Wizard |
| 31-33 | School Champion |
| 28-30 | Grade Level Champion |
| 25-27 | Best In The Class |
| 23-24 | Excellent Student |
| 20-22 | Good Student |
| 17-19 | Average Student |
| 0-16 | Better Luck Next Time |

## ANSWERS 1987-88 6TH GRADE CONTEST

| | | | | |
|---|---|---|---|---|
| 1. C | 9. C | 17. B | 25. B | 33. D |
| 2. C | 10. B | 18. C | 26. B | 34. B |
| 3. A | 11. C | 19. A | 27. C | 35. A |
| 4. D | 12. D | 20. D | 28. D | 36. D |
| 5. B | 13. A | 21. D | 29. A | 37. C |
| 6. D | 14. C | 22. D | 30. C | 38. C |
| 7. B | 15. B | 23. D | 31. B | 39. D |
| 8. A | 16. A | 24. A | 32. B | 40. C |

# RATE YOURSELF!!!
## for the 1987-88 6TH GRADE CONTEST

| Score | Rating |
|---|---|
| 36-40 | Another Einstein |
| 34-35 | Mathematical Wizard |
| 31-33 | School Champion |
| 28-30 | Grade Level Champion |
| 26-27 | Best In The Class |
| 23-25 | Excellent Student |
| 20-22 | Good Student |
| 16-19 | Average Student |
| 0-15 | Better Luck Next Time |

## ANSWERS 1988-89 6TH GRADE CONTEST

| | | | | |
|---|---|---|---|---|
| 1. B | 9. C | 17. A | 25. C | 33. B |
| 2. D | 10. B | 18. C | 26. A | 34. B |
| 3. C | 11. D | 19. D | 27. B | 35. C |
| 4. D | 12. B | 20. C | 28. B | 36. C |
| 5. B | 13. D | 21. D | 29. D | 37. B |
| 6. C | 14. B | 22. B | 30. D | 38. A |
| 7. C | 15. C | 23. B | 31. C | 39. D |
| 8. A | 16. A | 24. B | 32. C | 40. A |

# RATE YOURSELF!!!
## for the 1988-89 6TH GRADE CONTEST

| Score | Rating |
|---|---|
| 36-40 | Another Einstein |
| 33-35 | Mathematical Wizard |
| 31-32 | School Champion |
| 29-30 | Grade Level Champion |
| 26-28 | Best In The Class |
| 23-25 | Excellent Student |
| 20-22 | Good Student |
| 16-19 | Average Student |
| 0-15 | Better Luck Next Time |

## ANSWERS 1989-90 6TH GRADE CONTEST

| | | | | |
|---|---|---|---|---|
| 1. C | 9. B | 17. D | 25. C | 33. A |
| 2. B | 10. C | 18. C | 26. B | 34. A |
| 3. B | 11. A | 19. A | 27. D | 35. B |
| 4. D | 12. D | 20. C | 28. B | 36. C |
| 5. B | 13. B | 21. B | 29. D | 37. B |
| 6. A | 14. A | 22. A | 30. C | 38. C |
| 7. D | 15. D | 23. C | 31. D | 39. B |
| 8. A | 16. C | 24. B | 32. C | 40. A |

# RATE YOURSELF!!!
## for the 1989-90 6TH GRADE CONTEST

| Score | Rating |
|---|---|
| 38-40 | Another Einstein |
| 36-37 | Mathematical Wizard |
| 33-35 | School Champion |
| 30-32 | Grade Level Champion |
| 27-29 | Best In The Class |
| 24-26 | Excellent Student |
| 21-23 | Good Student |
| 18-20 | Average Student |
| 0-17 | Better Luck Next Time |

## ANSWERS 1990-91 6TH GRADE CONTEST

| | | | | |
|---|---|---|---|---|
| 1. A | 9. B | 17. A | 25. C | 33. B |
| 2. D | 10. C | 18. B | 26. C | 34. D |
| 3. D | 11. C | 19. C | 27. B | 35. D |
| 4. A | 12. B | 20. C | 28. B | 36. C |
| 5. B | 13. C | 21. D | 29. A | 37. B |
| 6. D | 14. A | 22. C | 30. A | 38. C |
| 7. B | 15. D | 23. B | 31. A | 39. C |
| 8. A | 16. A | 24. D | 32. D | 40. B |

# RATE YOURSELF!!!
## for the 1990-91 6TH GRADE CONTEST

| Score | Rating |
|---|---|
| 39-40 | Another Einstein |
| 37-38 | Mathematical Wizard |
| 34-36 | School Champion |
| 31-33 | Grade Level Champion |
| 29-30 | Best In The Class |
| 26-28 | Excellent Student |
| 23-25 | Good Student |
| 20-22 | Average Student |
| 0-19 | Better Luck Next Time |

# Math League Contest Books
## *4th Grade Through High School Levels*

Written by Steven R. Conrad and Daniel Flegler, recipients of President Reagan's 1985 Presidential Awards for Excellence in Mathematics Teaching, each book provides schools and students with:

- Contests designed for a 30-minute period
- Problems ranging in difficulty from straightforward to challenging
- Contests from 4th grade through high school
- Easy-to-use format

*1-10 copies of any one book: $12.95 each ($16.95 Canadian)*
*11 or more copies of any one book: $9.95 each ($12.95 Canadian)*

Use the form below (or a copy) to order your books

Name:_____

Address:_____

City:_____ State:_____ Zip:_____

| Available Titles | # of Copies | Cost |
|---|---|---|
| *Math Contests—Grades 5 & 6 (Vol. 1)* Contests from 1979-80 through 1985-86 | _____ | _____ |
| *Math Contests—Grades 4, 5, 6 (Vol. 2)* Contests from 1986-87 through 1990-91 | _____ | _____ |
| *Math Contests—Grades 7 & 8 (Vol. 1)* Contests from 1977-78 through 1981-82 | _____ | _____ |
| *Math Contests—Grades 7 & 8 (Vol. 2)* Contests from 1982-83 through 1990-91 | _____ | _____ |
| *Math Contests—High School (Vol. 1)* Contests from 1977-78 through 1981-82 | _____ | _____ |
| *Math Contests—High School (Vol. 2)* Contests from 1982-83 through 1990-91 | _____ | _____ |
| *Shipping and Handling* | | $3.00 |

*Please allow 4-6 weeks for delivery*          Total: $_____

☐ Check or Purchase Order Enclosed; *or*

☐ Visa / MasterCard # _____

☐ Exp. Date _____ Signature _____

Mail your order with payment to:
**Math League Press**
**P.O. Box 720**
**Tenafly, NJ 07670**

Phone: (201) 568-6328 • Fax: (201) 816-0125